THE FILMS

PICAS SERIES 40

Canadä

Guernica Editions Inc. acknowledges the financial support
of the Government of Canada through the Book Publishing Industry
Development Program (BPIDP).

MICHEL CHION

THE FILMS OF
JACQUES TATI

TRANSLATED BY ANTONIO D'ALFONSO

GUERNICA
TORONTO · BUFFALO · CHICAGO · LANCASTER (U.K.)
2003

Original Title:
Jacques Tati

A sincere thank you to Monique Viñas and Patrick Williamson without
whose collaboration this present translation would not have been possible.
A special thank you to Halli Villegas and Elana Wolff for the fine tuning.
I would like to dedicate this translation to my friend Luigi, with whom I
saw all of Tati's films.

Guernica Editions Inc.
P.O. Box 117, Station P, Toronto (ON), Canada M5S 2S6
2250 Military Road, Tonawanda, N.Y. 14150-6000 U.S.A.

Distributors:
University of Toronto Press Distribution,
5201 Dufferin Street, Toronto, (ON), Canada M3H 5T8

Gazelle Book Services, Falcon House, Queen Square,
Lancaster LA1 1RN U.K.

Independent Publishers Group,
814 N. Franklin Street, Chicago, Il. 60610 U.S.A.

Typesetting by Selina.
Printed in Canada.
Second Edition.
Legal Deposit – First Quarter
National Library of Canada
Library of Congress Card Number: 2002102765

Canadian Cataloguing in Publication Data
Chion, Michel
The films of Jacques Tati
(Picas series ; 40)
Translation of: Jacques Tati.
ISBN 1-55071-175-X
1. Tati, Jacques, 1909-1982. Criticism and interpretation.
I. Title. II. Series.
PN1998.3.T37C4813 2002   791.43'0233'092   C2002-900478-0

CONTENTS

FOR MY MOTHER

FOREWORD

Actor, scriptwriter, filmmaker and often producer, Jacques Tati is along with Chaplin one of the most well-rounded artists working in the medium of film. He paid a high price to acquire and then maintain this right. He shot six full-length films in thirty-five years – five of them being works of fiction. He refused attractive propositions, many from the U.S.A., because such offers would have forced him back to the narrow paths of traditional comedy.

Many feared that his films would suffer the fate reserved for the demanding genre that is comedy: his films would be admirable, but they would lose their power to seduce.

Tati was very much alive when a large portion of his audience deserted him after the release of *Playtime.* Nevertheless, the re-release of his first three films in France is reassuring. Tati's movies continue to draw laughter, tenderness and emotions from spectators of all walks of life that gather in our tiny fifty-seat theatres housed in modern, "functional," and uninhabitable complexes that could easily have been settings for *Playtime II.*

Tati had what it takes to bring together men and women who would (in real life or at the cinema) not naturally run into one another. Whenever one of his films gets shown, it is not unusual to find punks sitting, side by side, with sixty-year-old couples. Everyone becomes a Tati film buff, reminiscing together.

Such a scene would have made Tati happy. The coexistence of opposites was, at least for Tati, proof that he had not become obsolete.

Tati has not changed one bit. He is the wallflower critics forget to mention on their movie hit-parade charts. He is the misfit who is accidentally discovered and finally receives the recognition he so rightly deserves.

Tati considered himself a craftsman, but behaved like an artist. He disliked mass productions. He was not scared of disappointing his spectator. He risked everything whenever he offered what was least expected from him.

He worked slowly on his films. Once completed, he could view the film a hundred times until he found a detail that had gone unnoticed before. Tati was a perfectionist.

In *Playtime* he was an inventor; in *Trafic,* the photographer of stark reality. Tati endeavored to innovate technically, both visually and in his use of sound. Capable of drawing novel findings from old and fresh material, he stood at the opposite pole of "primitive filmmaker."

Throughout his lifetime, Tati perfected and refined the unique manner in which he made films. Few filmmakers handle cinema's hundred-year-old history with the same agility. When it comes to Tati, silent movies feel as modern as music videos. One dream he raved about but never fulfilled sums up what he wished most: to solder together various aspects of film history and present them in a daring spectacle. He also wanted to add sound tracks to silent movies so as to make them more accessible to a new generation of movie-goers.

There are various ways of approaching Tati. I have chosen to speak mostly about the filmmaker, the artist who in just six films created a complete and unique universe.

Following a short introduction, this freewheeling essay tackles questions of Tati's brand of comedy (Chapters 2 and 3); his use of dialogue and images (Chapters 4 and 5); his narrative system and the nature of the world he often revealed to us by his particular development of sound (Chapters 8 and 9); the messages conveyed through his depiction of the world (Chapter 10); the aesthetic dimension of his films (Chapter 11); and, finally, his manipulation of time (Chapter 12). Certain details from each films are used to illustrate these points, but these by no means represent an exhaustive catalog of Tati's genius. Tati wanted each spectator to create his or her own film while watching his and I have no intention of denying you this pleasure!

To conclude this introduction, I would like to express my gratitude to all those who helped me with their suggestions; they made the writing of this essay so much easier: in particular Madame Sophie Tatischeff, but also Charles Tatum Jr., Jean-Paul Fargier, Didier Kuntz and Christine Groult.

CHAPTER I

Arrival from . . .

"Vous avez bien reçu nos fleurs? Eh bien c'est l'essentiel."
("You did get the flowers. That's what counts.")
Mon Oncle

1

The sky is broader and wider than usual. Domineering. Dark blue. Orly stands under fleecy white clouds. The airport slowly comes alive, like in a film. Yes, just like in a film. I'm scribbling down these words at the very spot where *Playtime* begins: Orly-Sud. Would you believe me if I told you that this is a coincidence? The sort of coincidence Tati was a master at inventing.

What is it about this May 1st that compels me to write these notes? Skies in Tati's films are never as misty as they are today. Tati shies away from mist. His skies are bright; his air, clean and sharp.

Can this be "chance" then that I should be writing these sentences just as lily-of-the-valley vendors swarm about me, their countless little white bells multiplying under cellophane? Of course not.

At the end of *Playtime*, in the bus scene, the souvenir that the young American tourist carries on

her lap is a sprig of a lily-of-the-valley. It is the gift
that Hulot has given her: a flower so compact and
impersonal it seems man-made. The woman notices
that the flower resembles the bending street lamps
against the sky. We, too, notice the similarity. A suit-
able little flower that smells like bath soap, a gift
worthy of being offered to the quiet woman with
the toothy smile: an idyllic May flower, the kind
you find on postcards. Such are the auspices under
which this book begins.

Other signs appear: it is the first of May, Labour
Day, consequently a day tailor-made for Tati, who
made workdays holidays, and holidays workdays.
Were Tati to have been born in May, it wouldn't surprise us in the least.

In fact, he was born on October 9th, 1908. The
sky darkens. If you are Tati and destiny speaks, you
know it isn't just the blinking of an eye.

2

Playtime, Tati's fourth full-feature film, was completed in 1967. Tati said: "I went a little astray with
Mon Oncle, but soon made my way back to what I
really enjoy" (*Cahiers du cinéma,* No. 199, March
1968, p. 15). The meeting ground is an airport.

The waiting area is vast and quiet.

A bell rings. A plane lands. Here come the passengers, one by one, through customs.

A woman in a fur coat suddenly appears; she is
alone. An annoyed customs-officer comes towards
her: "Do you have anything to declare?" Vexed, the

woman opens her little handbag – the only thing she is carrying. She sums up the situation rather abruptly with a single word: "Stupid."

A short man with a moustache follows – a Marcel Dassault look-alike. He is assailed by a horde of journalists who ask him questions that the customs-officer asked earlier. This time, however, the words have a different meaning: "Can you declare something? Just a word?"

We only catch the muttering, the beginning of a sentence – "All I can tell you for the moment is . . ." – before he makes his way to the exit.

A name-tag clipped to his briefcase revolves like a propeller and flaps in time to his walk. This man might be short but he is the director of a large, important firm.

Later, we will notice him in a photograph hanging in a waiting room.

What does the woman declare?

A child? Stupid!

At the end of the sequence, Tati delivers a gag.

But is it a gag?

Whining echoes down the empty hall: a female American tourist turns and sees a woman, ill at ease, stroking a bag. Does the bag conceal a dog?

This tourist is one of the film's main characters: Barbara.

What should the man declare?

What crucial word should he utter?

"Just a word."

A voice on the loud-speakers announces who is arriving and who is departing.

Whose path will we cross?
Where is Hulot?

3

One could say that for Tati airports, hotels, restaurants are not normal public places where people
meet. No, people run into one another, but they
never really meet. No, no, these spaces are rooms
where people come into contact without anything
ever emerging from such encounters.

4

Let's go back to the beginning of *Playtime*. Before
the man makes his appearance. Earlier on, way
before the airport scene.

Sky and music: that's all there is. The cosmos.
And not a soul around to feel a thing.

The sky is broad, everywhere alive with color.
Now the modulation of music notes.

The music begins. A gentle hum, symphony of
air. The air issues an invitation to sparrows, messages, airplanes. And – as tradition has it – children.

In the background we hear faintly a celestial
choir.

The main building at the Orly airport, shot
from a low angle, comes alive. Two nuns sway by,
their cornets flapping in unison.

(Whenever people appear in a Tati film, they do
so in twos, like the two motorcyclists in *Trafic* or in

Mon Oncle, the angels of the road and guardians of the sky.)

For *Playtime,* Tati redesigned Orly to give it the appearance of a hospital clinic. Hence, the perfect cleanliness. Nuns flutter by; then a couple, the wife treating her husband like an invalid; finally, a nurse comforting a crying baby.

Still, there is not a single image of the protagonist. No Hulot in sight.

Look at the sky. See how broad and clear it is. It feels like spring, the sky is big with white clouds. There is a forecast of rain. In fact, for the duration of the film the weather will be just fine.

Rain didn't spoil Hulot's holidays in 1953, nor did raindrops perturb his long walks in 1958. Rain won't be glistening on the streets of *Playtime* either.

The window panes will be free of mist.

This one time, the man with the pipe won't be seen carrying his trademark umbrella.

And so will it be. Well, until Tati goes back to the land of his ancestors to shoot the last episode of his Hulotian adventure. It is only then that humidity will start to thicken the air and rain will begin to start falling again.

But first it is as if the air has to be cleansed.

Away with you, fog, fumes, chiaroscuros!

May the air be diaphanous so that the signs on posts can be clearly visible to our eyes.

Wipe clean the surface of the screen, so that we can see what signs will emerge from the road. Notice the traffic lights, the flickering lamps, the electric garage door whose photosensitive eye is activated by a dog's tail.

Someone whistles at you. You turn. You react. You're about to bang your head against a lamppost. Welcome to reality.

> If I look back at my films, I realize that the path I took has been, in my opinion, not too difficult. I went a little astray with *Mon Oncle*, but I soon made my way back to what I really enjoy doing. *Playtime* is closer in spirit to *Les Vacances de Monsieur Hulot* than to *Mon Oncle*. I felt quite at home shooting *Playtime*.

5

Beyond the films, beyond his characters, Tati is a world unto himself. This is a statement that cannot be said of many comic geniuses.

Take Chaplin, for example. Here is a great figure about whom Tati held mixed feelings. There is no Chaplin world, there are only Chaplin films. The same thing can be said about Keaton: his characters maintain a special relationship with the world they move in. Nevertheless their world is still very much ours too.

To create a universe cinematographically you must not only create your own "fauna," but also the planet where that fauna will grow. You must be able to regulate the amount of oxygen in the air and the cycle of the ocean tides. Beyond the narrative, everything must be specific and personified. This, Tati managed fully, and from his first feature-length film, *Les Vacances de Monsieur Hulot*. Let's examine Tati's cinematic universe.

6

Life is filled with homages to Tati. His films are difficult to find. Now that Tati has left us, we have to welcome all the ways life pays tribute to this comic genius.

Life, and filmmakers.

In *Sacrifice*, a postman tumbles down the winding road on a bike hitched up by a mischievous boy: this is how Tarkovski pays homage to Tati.

In *Roma*, Fellini, who was a friend of Tati, filmed two nuns with cornets flapping rhythmically: at first, this sign of respect was mistaken for plagiarism.

In *The Party*, Blake Edwards shoots a story that unfolds in one location and during one evening. This catastrophe of a party taking place in a Hollywoodian villa could very well be a wink from both the filmmaker and Peter Sellers to the Royal Garden sequence in *Playtime*.

David Lynch, maker of *Eraserhead* and *Blue Velvet*, quotes Tati as being among his favourite filmmakers; and in fact the Plastac Factory in *Mon Oncle* could fit naturally into any David Lynch creation.

People love and admire Tati. It would be untrue to say that Tati did not receive this well-deserved recognition: people mention Tati in the same breath as Chaplin and Keaton. American critics have written essays and books about him.

I know Icelanders who, before they came to study in Paris, had formed their idea of what France was thanks to Tati's films; they imagined the French as being people who talk, gesticulate a lot and who can hardly be understood. Once in France, they found the portrait of the French to be the very likeness of the film reality. (Post-war French cannot stand to see their image in paintings or caricatures.)

Publications such as *Hara-Kiri* and the work of Cabu, considered to be the painter par excellence of French *beaufs* (vulgar and narrow-minded chauvinists) and their 1970s urban lifestyle, testify to being fans of Tati.

Tati made our parents laugh.

But do Tati's films still make people laugh today?

I feel as though I have known the gags in *Jour de fête* or *Les Vacances de Monsieur Hulot* forever, having heard them as a child, a thousand times, or, rather, having "snatched" them from grown-ups at suppertime.

As a young child, I did not automatically understand Tati. At seven years old, I did not find *Les Vacances de Monsieur Hulot* funny at all. I did not grasp the nuances very well. Objects seemed distant on the screen. *Vacances* seemed to be a film without faces.

From my first viewing, only the final image comes back to mind: Hulot's silhouette gesticulating, running in circles against the light display of fireworks.

When *Mon Oncle* was released, I was older. I

enjoyed this film more and was able to understand quite well what it was all about. Its jolly, tinkling theme was a tune I felt I had heard forever. In those days we used to say about Tati: "I went to see *mon oncle* (my uncle)" or "Have you seen *mon oncle* (my uncle)?" as though we were speaking about a relative.

Here's a strange image I remember: the cart ride through the night. It seemed all the more enigmatic as it was on screen at the very moment I stepped into the theatre late, in the middle of a showing. (Never be late for a Tati film.)

Tati creates situations which begin or end right in the middle of the action. His stories are full of ellipses: fade-outs on the protagonist in grave difficulty and fade-ins again, the day after, back to normal. Nothing indicates the incident is over. Another day begins, and in the air lingers the memory of a disappearance which fills us with apprehension and guilt.

7

For the second time in *Playtime,* evening falls. In many films, evening goes unnoticed, but in Tati's films night is always noticeable.

Unity of the cosmos.

At the end of *Playtime,* Barbara notices the bells of the lily and then lampposts in the shape of lilies.

Urban flowers.

She smiles.

CHAPTER 2

Comic Democracy

"Eh bien Monsieur, on vous écrira, pour l'instant,
nous n'avons pas besoin d'acrobates."
("Thank you, sir, we'll be calling you. But for the
time being, we're not hiring acrobates.")

Mon Oncle

1

Here is how the press kit at the time of *Playtime*'s
release presented the film's complex storyline:

> Our futurist world turns quickly into a hellish labyrinth
> where Hulot, the sweet dreamer, can, unawares, sow
> total disruption!

Further on:

> Monsieur Hulot spreads panic . . . At the Royal Garden
> he spends an evening punctuated by the catastrophes he
> has triggered off . . .

This synopsis, at the very least supervised and perhaps even written by Tati himself, is neither faithful
nor relevant to the film. Blame is put on Hulot for
events he does not play any part in. These words

unfortunately exaggerate the seriousness of the out-come. There's nothing but typical panic in *Playtime*.

How can you defend a film by saying what it isn't? How can you say that Hulot is not the pro-tagonist of *Playtime*? Isn't he the one who triggers the handful of benign incidents? Isn't he responsible for everything that happens in the film?

Fortunately, today, we know that the uncon-scious is incapable of experiencing negation.

If the film is a constant and meticulous denial of the role of the protagonist and the catastrophes for which his very presence is responsible for sparking off, then Hulot and these catastrophes are indeed the subject of this study.

Would it have been sensible, as Tati wanted, to use Hulot, already popular with the audience, to draw us to the other characters and the film's set-tings?

Was it reasonable of Tati to introduce in the same film a character named Barbara, a female Hulot, a Hulotte as woolly as Hulot himself, in order to direct our curiosity elsewhere?

Certainly not.

As expected, the audience screamed for Hulot and his catastrophes!

Yet it is amazing that Tati could imprudently build, entirely construct his film, so to speak, on this fragile foundation.

We all know what happened next.

After *Playtime*'s commercial failure, Tati had the chance to make one more (and last) film, *Trafic*.

He accepted this offer with the tacit understanding that he would bring Hulot back to the screen.

In the script of his last film project entitled *Confusion*, Tati planned to kill off his protagonist.

He died first.

Yes, Tati is a protagonist and, fortunately for us, a glimpse of him as a protagonist still lingers on today.

2

Let us consider two gags, taken respectively from *Jour de fête* and *Les Vacances de Monsieur Hulot*.

Both start at the same point, and both find their essence in what will turn out to be the "logo" in *Trafic*: the straight road and the road that forks away.

François, the postman, rests his bike against a car. Suddenly the bike hurtles down the sloping path as the driver in the car drives away. Here comes the joke: instead of having the bike roll off into a ditch as the road curves, the bike is anthropomorphized. We watch it as it turns round the bend – exactly as François would have done had he still been riding it.

In *Les Vacances*, Hulot's car runs away as well. It freewheels on its own down a slope, two lady passengers in the back seat, too busy chatting away to notice that the car moving forward is without a driver! And now the twist. As the road ahead turns off into a curve, the car wanders off into the entrance of a private estate. This time the car does not turn, as we are led to expect, but boldly rides on into the estate, where the ladies are welcomed . . . by the owner's rifle shots!

After this unreal, burlesque moment, a second more realistic and "natural" gag follows.

> From the very beginning, all I have been trying to do . . . is to give elements of truth to comic characters (*Cahiers du cinéma*, No. 83, May 1958).

Truth? What does he mean by truth? What is this word doing here? Doesn't Tati realize film is fiction?

The fact is that he strongly believes in this word. It is a word he defends: Never go beyond the limits of plausibility.

It is too easy for comedies to leap over into the unreal world, and when they do, it is usually to the detriment of our enjoyment.

Tati bases his comedies on observation. He won't resort to "magical" gags anymore, such as the one in *Jour de fête,* when the bicycle without its driver rolls along and then comes to a full stop, all on its own, at the door of the bistro.

Tati makes a bargain with his audience about the type of comedy he promises and the sort of gags to be expected from him from now on. He rarely appeals to our vision, and when he does he asks so little from us. For instance, he juxtaposes fairground music to cars driving in circles at the end of *Playtime.* This sort of artistic restraint takes him a long way.

3

Tati brings about his little revolution in the art of
screen entertainment by giving the comic figure the
right to laugh, not the silly or aggressive laughter of
big Hardy when he is about to relish the funny
moment himself – but the observant, ironic, distant
laughter the spectator lets out when he catches a
flash involving another person.

During the funeral scene Hulot is mistaken,
despite himself, for a mourning relative. When people come to shake hands with him, murmuring their
condolences, he himself finds the situation funny
and starts to giggle nervously.

In the democracy of comedy to which this filmmaker tends (Tati makes each one of us into a
potential Hulot), the spectator and the characters
are given equal rights, as are the film "artisans."
Everybody is permitted to laugh and, in turn, be
laughed at.

This turnaround of the spectator has not always
been well received. In *Mon Oncle*, the workers at
Plastac break into a fit of laughter when they notice
the waste-pipes popping out of the machine, and in
so doing question our privilege as an audience to
laugh at them. Suddenly, we the audience are no
longer in a laughing mood.

Anxious about continuity, quite understandably,
Tati draws out the consequences of this never-end-
ing show.

There was a time when comedy consisted of the
universal one-man comic; later came the tandem act

of Laurel and Hardy, modeled on Coco-the-clown and the white clown; followed by the Marx Brothers who shared their gags with everyone; finally by Tati who brings comedy to its paroxysm by making every one of his numerous characters a potential comic.

The Marx Brothers, however, do not belong to the tradition of the single comic who attracts all the laughter; they lead us to the democracy of the comic as inaugurated by Tati. This, Tati is well aware of. The Marx Brothers are practical jokers who make people laugh at somebody else's expense – more at their antics than at their own expense.

The artist who breaks the mold does not have it easy. After *Playtime*, Tati's democratic comedy was rejected by a public that did not cherish its "everybody-is-funny" ingredient. Such an idea meant that Tati possessed a singular world view.

4

In *Les Vacances*, Hulot is made to fit into the pattern whereby he triggers off catastrophe. Yet gradually, film by film, Tati would abandon this technique.

By the time we get to *Playtime*, Hulot becomes responsible for one and only one catastrophe: he accidently tears off part of the ceiling of the Royal Garden restaurant; such an incident, however, eventually fades amid innumerable incidents that come about due to the faulty construction and hasty completion of the restaurant itself.

The Big Bust (La Grande Déglingue): had Gérard Oury directed this film, he would most certainly have used this title for the Royal Garden episode in *Playtime.* Even as fine a filmmaker as Blake Edwards used the "big bust" image when talking of *The Party.* Can we blame him? Absolutely not. Still, this is not the sort of fun Tati was trying to achieve.

Tati's restaurant scene is founded on the principle of "stock-taking" rather than accumulation. If we are looking for a character who records what unfolds in this scene, it would have to be the unhappy architect who, through his blunders, ends up being responsible for most of the disaster. He runs left and right, scribbling in his notebook the complaints that explode around him: from the waiters, the chef, the cloakroom lady, the owner, as well as the butler.

The kitchen hatch is too narrow for the dishes to pass through; pieces of the dance floor come loose; the air conditioning goes from extreme heat to extreme cold; the backs of chairs leave their crown motifs on the backs of customers; peoples' clothes tear as they catch on the panels.

In another film, these comic incidents would have been built up into general disorder. But this does not happen here.

One gag at the Royal Garden features the waiter-turned-scarecrow. The man tears his jacket and goes to stand in the wings of the restaurant. There he slowly inherits his co-workers' stained and spoiled clothes and accessories. This remarkable gag works on the idea of not only being repetitive but accumulative as well. The enclosed space fills with tension, events go haywire, and yet, strangely enough, there isn't much that accumulates, apart from the clothes that the waiters drop onto the waiter-turned-"coat-hanger."

It is obvious that Tati refuses overkill in this game of laughter. A gag should be successful on its own terms and preferably in a limited time span so that we can enjoy and appreciate it fully. And no earlier gag should rescue a forthcoming gag, either by foreshadowing it, or outbidding it. This peculiar comic style presupposes the disinvestment and reinvestment of reality. We are being asked over and over again to engage with the gag quickly and just as quickly disengage.

Tati frequently uses the "repetitive gag." For instance, in *Playtime*'s restaurant scene, the Turbot à la Royale is ten times seasoned but never served. Repetition, however, serves to express Tati's love for variation and is not aimed at helping the impact of the singular gag. On the contrary, with Tati, repetition tends to dilute gags; and Tati particularly cherishes gag dilution.

5

Noël Burch has wonderfully described how the non-linearity of "early" cinema enabled spectators to explore scenes as though they were complex surfaces. Before the advent of modern cinema with its codes of links, edits and cuts which sewed shots into a perfect whole, directors used general shots swarming with detail. There was an *autarchy* of shots in relation to other shots.

In passing, Burch notes that Tati is among the rare directors of the Talkies who took up this method of depicting reality.

Dramas would eventually come up with their own filmic conventions: every sign – character, setting, plot line – with which the shot is loaded, is organized into a hierarchy. Some choose imagery; others substance; all propel the spectator to lose himself in an exclusive and central point of view: the plot unfolding.

In his non-dramatic, slow-moving films, all shot at a distance, Tati takes his time, without over-emphasis, to spread out images, gags and characters over the entire surface of the screen.

Through different means than those used by Visconti, Antonioni or Wenders, Tati crosses into the tradition of cinema as novel, whereby the complete fabric of notations and sensations is revealed. As Barthélémy Amengual accurately puts it in his excellent study on "Monsieur Tati's strange humor":

> We could say that Tati replaces the burlesque serial with the novel (for example, *Jour de fête*). In the novel, everything that the story loses in the basic plot, the writer gains in inner life. Indeed, Tati keeps his gags to a minimum and slows down their pace, whipping up an

intellectual froth around each gag and filling his characters with ambiguity; he makes life difficult for any character who might seem above it all (*Cahiers du cinéma*, No. 32, February 1954, p. 33).

6

As to the matter of style, Tati is daring and flexible with concepts. Like Chaplin, he is keen on having complete control over every facet of his work. Fearful of being considered old-fashioned and dreading the natural aging process which usually comes to films through the musical score, he would often redo the sound track and the music score of his films – the only elements that could still be modifed years after filming. Tati would endlessly, and willingly, remix and recut all his films, as is the case for *Les Vacances*.

Tati has audacious ideas on the possibility of altering the volume of the sound track during the presentation of a film – much like the effective applications in concrete music – which indicates to what extent film is, for Tati, an "interactive" medium, to use current theoretical jargon.

In the field of comic cinema (which he distinguished from comedy), Tati chooses to be original on all levels, and quickly becomes so. By the time he gets to his second full-length film, Tati is no longer willing to make concessions to traditional methods of doing things, if they do not suit him.

Has the public acknowledged Tati's originality?

This is far from certain. The public and critics alike tend to minimize his originality and insist more on what he has in common with traditional comedy.

His obsession for being original is in no way naive or off-the-cuff. Everything is conscious, thought-over, and openly admitted. Tati knows what he is doing and what he is not doing. Such an attitude is rare, especially with a person so adept on all levels. This does not necessarily make things easier for him and for his evolution as an artist. When you are aware of what you are doing and become a master at doing it in a short period of time, what else can you expect from yourself? You attempt to surprise yourself.

7

Tati's first two full-length films still respect the golden rule of comedy. Both films offer the final "chase" sequence: in *Jour de fête* there is the postman's round *à l'Américaine* and at the end of *Les Vacances* we have Hulot's entanglements with fireworks which channel the spectator's gaiety into a collective and global burst of laughter.

Already by the third film, *Mon Oncle,* Tati gives us a less flashy decrescendo. However, as the major part of the film is classically and strongly built, such an ending does not spoil its success.

With its satirical view of the modern world, *Playtime* treats us to a finale that is more melancholic, leaving us with an array of varied emotions.

At the end of the film, the traffic jam gag at the roundabout is quietly humorous, not ostentatious.

Tati works with deft touches: the collective euphoria released by the long, spectacular restaurant sequence has plenty of time to fade. This undoubtedly is what Tati wants. The last fifteen minutes of *Playtime* immerses each spectator in personal solitude before he walks out of the cinema back into reality. It is possible that such an ending is responsible for the film's failure with the public.

Jour de fête (1949) has been criticized for being inconsistent in construction and tone. This film is divided into two nearly independent sections: the first part tells the chronicle of a tiny village in France that comes alive with the arrival of the fair; the second part is the round *à l'Américaine* of a barely efficient postman, which soon turns into a Keaton-like burlesque comedy.

More refined in style, Tati's second full-length film, *Les Vacances de Monsieur Hulot,* features a succession of scenes and short moments about summer vacation on a peaceful Normandy beach. Tati has no hesitation about giving the daring and disparate *Vacances* a blend of playfulness and refinement. Nevertheless, Tati runs up against the real problem of form with *Mon Oncle.*

Of all Tati's films, *Mon Oncle* (1958) is the one film that conforms to the rules of traditional narrative. This work represents the only example of the filmmaker's efforts to genuinely carry the story to its end, thanks to a succession of causes and effects.

Hulot, an unsettled misfit, lives in a quaint and

picturesque part of town, whereas the Arpels live in an ultra-modern villa. His sister, Madame Arpel, is intent on finding a wife for her brother, and convinces her jealous husband to find Hulot a job: Monsieur Arpel does not appreciate Hulot's influence on his son Gérard. Both initiatives fail miserably. *Mon Oncle* details the goals and wishes of a cast of characters who fail. Yet there is one success story: the son Gérard grows closer to his father.

Something, however, in this great construction escapes, crumbles and, in the opinion of many critics, drags on: the scene of the misshaped pipes popping out of the Plastac factory, the result of a blunder committed by Hulot, whose job it is to keep an eye on them. There is no doubt that these metres of cumbersome plastic pipe serve a purpose: to show us Hulot's ineptitude for work. (How *does* Hulot make a living? Three of the four films in which he appears leave this a total mystery.) This pipe-drama directs us outside the story proper. The spectator seems stuck within this sequence, and it is precisely here that the screenplay sinks and the narrative derails irretrievably.

On the visual level, *Mon Oncle* is a testimony of Tati's evident obsession with graphic design. Compared to the joyful, skilful untidiness and unstructured images of *Les Vacances,* with its characters made to develop sympathetically in awkward settings, *Mon Oncle* seems to be a slideshow of beautiful settings organized by a designer.

Playtime (1967) portrays a Paris so modern that it is unrecognizable. Here again, Tati reveals his obsession with visual form, but this time he has freed himself of the tics and errors found in his preceding film.

8

Playtime is, especially in its first part, a film made through process of elimination.

Gone is everything superfluous: settings are bare, smooth, colossal. What is said about Hulot's family? Nothing. No word on his sister or brother-in-law, nothing on his nephew or house. Hulot appears from nowhere and is going nowhere.

Gone are the protagonist and the plot: here is a perfectly circular screenplay meant to wake up a world of repetition with discreet waves.

Gone are traditional dramatic devices: there is nothing to conquer; nothing to assert; no skin to defend, no castration to live through. Lazy characters on holiday disappear and reappear; no ID anywhere.

Gone is nature: not a blade of grass, not a breath of sea air is left. The sounds of animals, so abundant in *Jour de fête* and even in *Trafic*, are totally left out: a rooster, the only animal to have escaped the slaughterhouse, crows absurdly at dawn in a setting of buildings, for the few haggard survivors coming out of a night club.

Gone is Paris: even though this is where the story takes places: whatever remains of the city can be seen as a reflection ("ideas") on window panes.

Here, the ghost of the Eiffel Tower; there, Montmartre, as fleeting as the town of Ys, which legend has it, has vanished.

Gone is color: colors were bright and gaudy in *Mon Oncle*; in *Playtime* they are sucked dry by a kind of gigantic syringe; symbols are all that remain, streetlights in an ocean of greyish blue steel . . .

There is not a speck of dust anywhere, not even the dust Madame Arpel assiduously sweeps away with her dust-filled dusters at the beginning of *Mon Oncle*: it is as though a giant feather-duster, worthy of the maddest dreams of Hulot's obsessional sister, has removed even the smallest particles of dust from all the settings.

The need to simplify in *Playtime* is obvious. And whatever fat has been cut out has nothing to do with films made by other directors; only comparisons to Tati's own preceding film are valid, and to the rules *Mon Oncle* established. These films complement one another, are unified by some superior rhythm.

Nevertheless, *Playtime* inevitably sends us back to *Les Vacances*, revisited twelve years later. We notice a semantic resonance in the titles and subject matter; both films deal with pastimes. But where have the sea and beach gone to? Oh, they are still there, but now they have been sublimated in names (Strand-Plage, in German), in those signs nailed on doors of highrises, in the sounds and melodies, such as the Hawaiian song broadcast in the air-conditioned lounge, in the muffled throbbing of cars outside apartment buildings.

Trafic (1971) is dictated by outside circumstances which Tati has to agree to if he wishes to shoot another film. *Playtime* is a commercial failure. People are demanding that Tati bring Hulot back under the limelight. Tati is forced to respect the conditions imposed by his Dutch co-producer.

Trafic turns out to be as impure a patchwork as *Playtime* was pure and intransigent. Nonetheless, it is an endearing film for different reasons: we are invited to a picaresque journey of a man who leaves Paris to go to Amsterdam for a car show, but arrives much too late to participate.

Contrary to *Playtime*, which is built on the principle of selection and exclusion, *Trafic* is founded on the concept of acceptance: everyone is welcome and everything gets shuffled around: urban and rural life, earth and sky, man and woman, extremely structured images and neo-realist scenes. The plot of the film takes us everywhere, moving from one place to another, as we move through loosely connected incidents.

The conditions under which the film is directed and produced can only be partially to blame for the outcome. Tati seems more relaxed, more in touch with his bucolic nature. He places the camera on the bank of a canal and films cars that are driving by – many scenes are not even staged. In other words, it is as though he has just discovered people in real life. In fact, the people in *Trafic* appear to be more alive and have more presence than those in *Playtime*.

The owner of the garage (Tony Keepers) where the story leads us at one point is stunningly natural in his colorful and messy home. How can we forget this man who says nonstop that he can repair anything ("I fix everything")? He abruptly and cordially goes berserk as he searches everywhere for some instrument in his chaotic jumble, throwing aside unwanted tools, a miaowing cat, and anything else he puts his hand on. And how can we forget the short, masochistic, depression-prone boss in *Trafic* (played by Honoré Bostel), who complains without end and often breaks into recriminations. He is a far more profound and human character than Arpel in *Mon Oncle,* who is nothing more than a caricature.

Giffard, Schultz, Reinhart, Schneider, the bosses, the employees, the doormen, the barmen, the workers – the characters in *Playtime* – are just pencilled-in and abstract figures, crushed by modern urban architecture.

The men and women in *Trafic* have run away from *Playtime*'s cold and dry prison where they were forced to make us laugh. *Playtime* is as conceptual as a musical score. *Trafic,* even if more uneven, is full of vitality and sensuality.

Tati's evolution is not linear; whenever balance is achieved, it remains precarious.

If *Playtime* sends us back to *Les Vacances*, *Trafic* leads much deeper into the past, sharing a smile of complicity with *Jour de fête*. Once again with this film we are asked to rediscover roads, nature, cows, trees, and meadows. Hulot, now playing a graphic artist, ultimately echoes the landscape painter we first meet in *Jour de fête*.

It is easy after the fact to agree with Tati's own

negative criticism of the essential film *Mon Oncle* became; easy, too, to consider this film a partial failure because it sticks too closely to the rules of traditional satire. Critics, who were usually kind and knowledgeable about his films, such as Noël Burch or François Truffaut, felt likewise.

We wonder why Tati, after having received international recognition with *Les Vacances*, would decide to make *Mon Oncle* the way he did, especially when we consider that he was given complete freedom to make the film of his dreams.

Should we see here a sign on his part of wanting to belong to the world of mainstream cinema? Should we construe this as a weakness or a mistake? Is it wrong to believe that, from time to time, even Tati felt the need to move his humor away from the margins and closer to popular cinema?

After the fact, it is always easy to speak of a coherent body of work and stress how one film is better than another, or how one film is more original, more "magical" and miraculously so, than the others. When we do so, however, we minimize the quality of the less revolutionary works, which nevertheless helped produce the more successful films. We all try, as best as we can, to fit a variety of films into a single continuity, and to find a continuity that links not only all the films of a single artist, but also the works of one artist to the works of artists working in every genre.

Had Tati not made *Mon Oncle*, he would have been condemned to remake *Les Vacances*, and not necessarily with success.

What does Tati have to say about this experience?

A few words: "I went astray."

Exactly.

Each one of his films teaches us that the only way to get somewhere, anywhere, is by going astray.

9

In *Jour de fête*, François is summoned by one of his colleagues to watch an American documentary film. Later, when he comes out of the bistro, it is as though he were hallucinating: he is dazzled by the balloon held by a child. He is drunk, and the balloon becomes an apparition, his star of Bethlehem, his celestial vision.

In *Playtime*, a drunk is thrown out of the Royal Garden dancing-restaurant. On leaving the place, the man is seized by the sight of a neon arrow which points back to the entrance. As if coiled into an arc that becomes an arrow, the man follows the steadily flickering dots, turns round on himself and, guided by the arrow, re-enters the restaurant as the Saint of Saints. The Royal Garden is a metaphor for Paradise. If there are problems with reservations, they are ultimately linked to mercy and destiny.

When Arpel protects himself in his house behind a rigorously designed garden, he often displays, as Georges Sadoul has pointed out, the manners and attitudes of a monarch in Versaille: the allusion to splendor can be noticed in the fish-fountain. In *Playtime,* the metaphor of royalty achieves its paroxysm in the extraordinary episode of the Royal Garden. The designer of this "Jardin Royal" is certainly aware of the connotations behind the use of such prestigious terms. Even the backs of the chairs have been designed to culminate in a five-point crown.

As the evening of the inauguration unfolds, we see more and more women receiving the stamp of these crowns, which the seats imprint on their bare skin, or on their partners' jackets. Yet not all clients are honored with these stamps; Schultz (Billy Kearns), the life and soul of the party, uses these stamps as a rite of passage of sorts. In a decrepit corner of the restaurant Schultz has converted into a private club, he admits only those whose backs bear the "mark": an ambiguous symbol that falls somewhere between the stamp of infamy (Milady in *Les Trois Mousquetaires*) and the mark of being chosen.

We find a similar mark twice elsewhere.

In *Playtime*, a priest reading his breviary is unaware of the neon "o" (the "o" in the word "Drugstore") shining above his head: a halo that brings him closer to the world above. It is in heaven that we find whatever is needed to keep us moving forward: a sign of our being chosen.

In *Trafic*, why is Hulot sacked from Altra by his boss? Because Hulot is standing at the entrance of the exhibition hall looking at a worker perched on a ladder, whistling away as he is dismantling the huge "o" of the word "Salon." Hulot gets blamed for the man's whistling.

These signs are crowns that travel from one person to another, instead of remaining on a single head. It is Tati's objective to allow the halo of the chosen to journey over the common people's heads. In fact, this anarchy constitutes his comic democracy.

CHAPTER 3

Hulotus Errans

"Monsieur, je m'excuse, mais vous n'êtes pas Monsieur Hulot."
("I beg your pardon, sir, but you are not Monsieur Hulot.")

Playtime

1

We could sum up the singularity of Tati's genius as an actor by characterizing him as a comic with a big stature. Placed diametrically opposite to Chaplin's little man's body – the "little fellow" whose body was totally intent on expressing itself, Hulot possesses the kind of stature that needs some hiding place where it won't be bending over others. What sort of comedy can one do with such a tall body?

When he stands upright, Tati seems to have his head in the clouds. When he appears on the top floor of a building, he is presented – the gag is repeated twice in *Jour de fête* – with his head popping out of the window: as in the café he has just entered, catastrophically on his bike. Perhaps, it isn't a coincidence if Hulot lodges, both in *Les Vacances* or *Mon Oncle*, close to the rooftops.

While in real life Tati did not have the actual

size his films suggest (according to his daughter, he measured one metre eighty-three), Hulot is nonetheless perceived as a being tall man. His comedy is based on the fact that he has a tall, strong body.

2

The image we normally have of Hulot, his identikit portrait, is of a tall man, pipe in mouth, in too-short trousers and striped socks. Always properly dressed, Hulot is seen in a suit or sports clothes. He wears a bow tie or open collar, a too-short raincoat or a summer jacket. He often raises his hat courteously, and is armed with an umbrella. His walk is unique. He advances in big determined strides, as if carried by a force over which he has no say, and then suddenly he hesitates and falls into a sort of waltz that complicates his movement forward. Hulot never really stands at rest. Even when he is not moving, it is as though he were ready to move. He is a human turntable. We never know how to interpret his expressions always partially concealed by his pipe, his hat or the distance Tati imposes between Hulot and his spectators. He looks worried, stupid, but neutral. His attitude as well as his gestures confer on him a detached appearance – if you can call it that. In reality, there is something about Hulot that we are never quite able to define.

3

Laurel and Hardy are known as Stan and Ollie in the U.S.A., but as Dick and Doof in Germany. Buster Keaton was nicknamed "Malec" in France. In the case of Hulot, he is simply known in all countries as Monsieur Hulot. He is inseparable from the name he is given.

From the moment Hulot walks into the world, a powerful draft accompanies him into the hotel where he arrives. He is immediately asked to state his name. (We are reminded of the arrival of the invisible man in James Whale's film.) When the gag occurs in *Les Vacances de Monsieur Hulot*, he has his pipe stuck in his mouth and is unable to pronounce his name properly. He utters something that sounds like "Uuu-ooo." The hotel manager automatically pulls the pipe out of Hulot's mouth, and we finally hear the missing consonant. "H-u-l-o-t." The reception clerk himself repeats Hulot's name while he scribbles it down in the registry. This will be the only utterance he will speak throughout the film.

The surname Hulot is common France. It can easily be found in the phone book. But it is also found in Balzac's *La Cousine Bette,* where we are told about a certain Baron Hulot, who is a director at the War Ministry and the brother of a general. Tati may have borrowed it from an architect he once knew, whose gait, it was said, was somewhat peculiar.

The surname triggers a host of associations.

Hulot easily evokes the word *hublot* (porthole), which we encounter in *Mon Oncle*. It also brings to mind the nocturnal predator known in France as *hulotte* (the tawny owl).

Hulot's sister's house has two portholes *(hublots)* which at night light up like a pair of eyes, or more precisely, owl's eyes.

Hulot is a name that immediately sets off an alarm (albeit a very sonorous alarm at that). There is also an old French word *huler*, the name of another night bird.

But we also think of sight – which is not surprising. When viewing a film by Tati, be on the look out for these amusing details – always essential for the appreciation of his films.

The sound of Hulot also reminds us of the gibberish emitted by the loudspeaker at the railway station, the gurgling sounds we hear at the beginning of *Les Vacances*, which direct entire families to move from platform to platform, which finally is a phatic *"Hello, hello."*

Can we say that Hulot is a *phatic* name?

It seems to be for someone who hardly ever speaks and chokes on the few words that he does manage to utter, words we grasp only if Hulot himself is in the foreground. Otherwise, if he is at a distance, all we see is Hulot involved in some lively but silent discussion.

What a contrast Hulot is to Tati's real family name, which is filled with harsh consonants and an imperative third syllable: Jacques Tatischeff.

So much for the surname.

Let's ask ourselves a question nobody ever thinks of asking: What is Hulot's given name?

He doesn't seem to have one. We know him simply as "Monsieur Hulot."

4

Compare the effect the title would have if it were *Les Vacances de Hulot* (promiscuity, familiarity) with that of the film's actual title, *Les Vacances de Monsieur Hulot*. By adding *Monsieur Hulot*, Tati introduces an important social factor into his film: the outsider. It is this element of being an outsider that actually defines our hero.

Hulot represents, thanks to his physical appearance, a dramatic break with the village fool of *L'École des facteurs* and *Jour de fête*. The postman was so popular that producers begged Tati to make sequels, something to the effect of *Retour du facteur* (The Postman Strikes Back), *Facteur à New York* (The Postman in New York) and *Facteur se marie* (The Postman Gets Married).

The postman in *Jour de fête* is known on a first-name basis; he does not have a surname. Hulot is, on the contrary, a surname without a first name.

Hulot is the guy you recognize because he was in the same barracks as you, even though he never became a close friend. He gives you the illusion of familiarity, which really doesn't exist. He develops into a real person only when you bump into him by accident one night. Shopkeepers find him friendly. They greet him with a *"Bonjour"* or *"Au revoir, Mon-*

sieur Hulot." If people at the hotel are quick to ask him his name, it is because he has the face of someone they have met at school or in the army. His sister would naturally call him by a nickname, yet she, who remains nameless, avoids doing this.

François the postman is the scapegoat for his fellow citizens. He is the butt of practical jokes, public irony, and the target of the travelling fairground people.

By creating Hulot, Tati aims to re-establish a distance. From the start, Hulot is someone who exists only in the eyes and mouths of the beholder. He is someone who awakens suspicion or amused attention. *"Regarde, Monsieur Hulot!"* ("Look, it's Mr. Hulot!")

Thanks to Hulot, Tati breaks away from the pattern of having funny characters which we the audience dress up with nicknames the moment we cross the barrier of formality that separates reality from fiction.

Hulot is not the kind man the spectator would casually slap on the back.

Going from François the postman to Hulot, we move from the reality of a dissatisfied and restless man to that of a quiet man who seems only too anxious to re-integrate himself into society.

François is a grumbler; continually ratty, he bears a grudge against the Americans, the children who persecute him, his bike, the world and the ways of the universe.

Hulot, on the other hand, neither complains nor moans.

5

Hulot is a blurred man, a passer-by, a *Hulotus errans*. In *Playtime*, he is no longer "Monsieur Hulot." Rootless, he is sill recognized by people on the street, and three times at that: by two colleagues from his army days – his friend Marcel and the jolly Schneider (the former of working-class origin, and the latter a small boss) – and also by Giffard, the worker Hulot tried in vain to contact the morning of his escapade in the highrise.

At first Giffard does not pay Hulot much attention, but then, in the evening, he more than willingly engages him in a conversation.

If people are to approach Hulot, they must have met him once before.

Conversely, several times in the film, a stranger is mistaken for Hulot. When Giffard is out in search of Hulot, he mistakes him for an Englishman, an African-European man and then a man with a beard.

Eventually Hulot is reduced to being a ghost, as when Giffard catches Hulot's reflection in the window of the highrise.

Critics report that Tati, while working on *Playtime,* repeated a remarkable comment Bazin made in 1953. Hulot is a man "inclined to be":

> The originality of the character, as compared to those found in traditional Commedia dell'arte which lead to the burlesque, lies in this idea of non-completion. The hero in the Commedia dell'arte represents comic

essence; his function is clear and always identical to himself. On the contrary, Monsieur Hulot's main characteristic lies in daring not to be there entirely. He is a mobile inclination, the discretion of being. He raises shyness to the height of an ontological principle (*Qu'est-ce le cinéma*, Paris: Éditions du Cerf, 1975, p. 43).

Coming into contact with Hulot means that Giffard and Reinhart will come out of it injured: one breaks his nose while pursuing one of Hulot's doubles; the other breaks his glasses while shaking hands with Hulot.

The consequence of coming into contact with such a catastrophe prone creature is catastrophe, for our senses, especially our eyes. Should we be surprised?

6

Hulot, who is so shy and discreet in his love life, cannot be said to be totally devoid of sexuality.

On two occasions we catch Hulot revealing his mischievousness.

In *Mon Oncle*, during the garden party, Hulot sets about telling stories to the assembled audience which, judging by the reactions of the women present, can only be construed as being bold.

"Actually," we hear Hulot say to the lady next to him, "I'll tell you a short one." Hulot bends over and whispers into the lady's ear.

She utters a shocked "Oh!"

At the end of *Playtime*, Hulot wants to offer a farewell gift to Barbara who is about leave. He asks an arrogant-looking cheese seller installed at the entrance to a supermarket for "Frivolity, please?"

Hulot's sketchy love life has a distinctly Anglo-Saxon flavor. He finds reciprocity in *Les Vacances* in a friendly, elderly English lady who seeks his company.

In *Mon Oncle*, the neighbor Hulot's sister wants him to marry is an Anglophile snob, who is a kind person all the same.

Again, in *Playtime*, as in *Trafic*, the heroines are Americans.

With Hulot, women frequently pose as temptresses. The house-keeper's daughter tries to charm him by showing herself off in her Sunday best and by sitting on the luggage-rack of his motorcycle.

Barbara leans on Hulot as she slips her shoe back on. This gesture might have happened earlier at the Royal Garden when they were dancing together, but Tati chooses instead to have Hulot disappear.

In *Trafic*, it is Maria who takes the decisive first steps.

7

CLANG goes the now famous swinging door of the restaurant room in *Les Vacances*. Door stories are scattered throughout Tati's films. There is the door gag in the cloakroom scene in *Parade* and the glass door of the Royal Garden which flies to pieces when Hulot runs into it nose first. Elsewhere, we have Giffard running into a door which leaves him with a bandage on his nose and the door intact. Then there is the two-way door at customs in *Trafic*: Hulot knocks, but the person who says "Come in" is on the same side of the door as him. The door at the Arpel residence in *Mon Oncle* becomes a true obsession, both visually and sound-wise. In *Mon Oncle,* Hulot gets the door slammed twice in the face.

No matter what happens, Hulot keeps wanting to come back home, a home that is not his own. Why does he wander about trying to walk into as many houses as he can? The basic story of *Mon Oncle* can be read as a long walk back to the Arpel villa.

When Hulot brings his nephew Gérard back to his parents, he hardly dares to step into the garden. With time, he plucks up courage and, invited by his sister and brother-in-law, he gets to visit the kitchen. In a later scene, we find Hulot prowling around at night to mend the broken espalier tree.

Having brought Gérard home, Hulot decides to sleep, in the absence of the Arpels, on the living-room sofa. It is as though he has finally attained his goal. Indeed, the film comes to its end soon after this episode.

In *Jour de fête*, François who is by now quite drunk starts to deliver the mail in the middle of the night, which the villagers welcome with gun shots. They mistake him for a prowler.

If Hulot hangs around places where people invite him to their houses, these same people later chase him out. There are plenty of examples of this admission/eviction based plot: Hulot is thrown out by some (Arpel, the lady of the S.D.R.C., Reinhart, the manager of Altra), and is adopted or snapped up by others (Marcel, Schneider, the owner of the Saint-Maur bistro, the merry campers in *Les Vacances*). He finds himself left on the doorstep (by the Dutch lady in *Trafic* whose husband he will later drive back home).

Hulot is always standing "behind doors." On both sides of course: walking in or walking out.

As we will see, we also encounter the flipside of this inside/outside paradigm. Because we are never quite sure where an entrance is to be found, a paradox soon arises: How can Hulot be thrown out, if he was not allowed to come in?

Tati answers this question, but as with all his answers, this one is as convoluted as the question itself.

Think back to Reinhart Koldehoff's display stand in *Playtime*. (In *Mon Oncle*, Hulot gets sacked from S.D.R.C. before he actually starts working.) Koldehoff is the German owner of a firm whose product at the Salon is being promoted as the "silent door." The company's slogan is: *Slam your doors in a golden silence.*

Koldehoff mistakes Hulot for one of those "false Hulots" planted like decoys throughout the film. This Hulot look-alike is accused by Koldehoff's partner as being the man who a few moments before was nosing about in the company's private desk drawers. Koldehoff tries to express his anger to Hulot but can't. He becomes the victim of his own obsession for silent doors. Koldehoff knows of only one way to vent his anger and that is, by kicking Hulot out of his stand. But how will he manage this in an office that is an open display stand? A stand with doors that are there for promotional purposes only? A tricky thing to do. All the more so if one considers the fact that Hulot is neither an employee, nor an intruder on Koldehoff's territory.

Consequently, and here lies the wit of the situation, Koldehoff must first invite Hulot into his stand before he can throw him out. Koldehoff begs an astonished Hulot who does not understand: *"Ah, monsieur, entrez, ne vous gênez pas"* ("Oh, please, sir, do come in, make yourself at home"). Koldehoff pulls Hulot up onto the stand. He politely takes his hat and coat, and hangs them on a coat hanger, placed to make one feel at home. Koldehoff invites Hulot to sit down. Hulot does as he is told to do.

Hulot says nothing. Koldehoff becomes desperate, loses his temper and, finding no other way to release his anger, slams the miracle door. The door shuts forcibly without making a noise.

What lies on the other side of this door? Nothing. Does the door open up to a mysterious place, such as Hulot's bedroom which we never see?

Hulot, who has heard nothing, turns around, surprised to see Koldehoff gone. Strange. This disappearing act is something we normally associate with Hulot!

8

A scene from *Les Vacances*.

This happens right after Hulot has fallen into
the sea, his kayak folded in two. Summoned by the
lunch bell, Hulot runs to the hotel, totally soaked.
He wipes his feet on the doormat, quite laughably,
and tiptoes towards the hall, leaving behind muddy
footprints. An officer stands in his way who, too
busy explaining his military exploits to the English
woman, does not notice an embarrassed Hulot running and hiding among the garments on a coat-
stand nearby.

This action results in footprints leading up to
the officer, who finally notices the stains on the
floor. Though he is certain that his shoes are dry, he
shakes his feet nonetheless, spouting: "I don't know
*si vous vous rappelez les Ardennes en temps de
guerre . . .*" And off goes the officer with his story.

The waiter becomes aware of the mud on the
floor, and immediately suspects the officer. But as
the officer slowly makes his way to the restaurant,
he leaves the waiter with the realization that the
footprints could not have possibly been made by the
military man. The footprints lead to the coat-stand!

The waiter goes to rummage about the coats.

Suddenly we hear the sound of footsteps.

By the time the waiter turns about, Hulot has
vanished, stamping a path of mud on the staircase
all the way to the bedrooms.

It is the sound of Hulot's footsteps that has
mysteriously printed itself on the floor.

Later Hulot reappears at his attic window, unseen and unheard, a refuge up in the clouds.

More than once, Tati has Hulot appearing and disappearing in a similar way – swallowed by a hole of absence that soon spits him out.

Compare what we have just seen to a true story told by Tati as an example of great comedy:

> Mme Tati's uncle owned a small country house near Dreux. The house had a very large garden . . . Let me tell you how a gag gets created. Dinner over, we go to the living room, six or seven of us, to play cards. Then a man, humble and kind, stands up and says: "I'm very sorry, but I can't stay. I have to get up early tomorrow morning." He leaves. It is raining hard, there is a terrible storm. Half an hour later, and I'm not inventing this, there's a knock at the door. We get slightly anxious and wonder, Who can that be? Someone opens the door, and who is there behind the door but the charming little man drenched to the bone. He says in a calm, polite voice: "Please forgive me, but can you help me find the way out?" That sort of thing gets the spectator's imagination rolling.

Tati shares a similar moment with us when he has Hulot disappear in *Playtime*.

It is evening. Hulot leaves Schneider's glass house. Schneider had invited Hulot in for a drink. The new building that Schneider has recently moved into has an entrance hall of large windows that appears on the left on the screen.

Schneider hears a noise and walks out to the entrance hall, turns on the light and laughs hilariously.

Hulot is standing there, unable to find the electric button that operates the door out.

The spectator who was led to believe that Hulot had left a long time before starts wondering: What could Hulot have been doing all this time in the dark, on the left side of the screen, struggling with the door as the story moved on?

How does Tati allow Hulot to vanish like that? How does he manage to make us forget Hulot?

Here's a possible answer to the riddle.

While Hulot is being taken to the door, Tati keeps our attention on a couple walking on the street from left to right in the foreground, busily arguing about a failed rendezvous. The camera whets the spectator's curiosity by panning along with the couple for a moment. Then abandoning the couple, the camera frames the building once more, pushing Hulot out into the left off-screen in the building's hallway.

Then the camera awakens the audience's sense of voyeurism. We are shown the interior of the two adjoining apartments. On the left, Schneider undresses in his room for the night while watching TV. On the right, Mme Giffard appears mesmerized by a TV show as well.

By a strange play of perspective, the wall separating both apartments becomes invisible and what we have is Mme Giffard wholly engrossed in the sight of Schneider pushing down his suspenders.

This explicitly erotic scene makes Hulot's ellipse possible. Though the scene might be a parody, it is certainly not without significance.

9

One thing Tati has never failed to do is refuse us the pleasure of identifying ourselves with the characters on screen.

Yet he will never invent a new protagonist like Hulot. Perhaps this is why he diminishes Hulot's importance by reducing him to a mere vector in his films.

When asked to make a sequel to the postman's adventures in *Jour de fête*, Tati refuses. He comes up with Hulot instead.

Because the public cries for more of Hulot, Tati should naturally start thinking of a third character. He doesn't.

He chooses the crazy and hopeless challenge of pitting Hulot against Hulot. He sets him off course and loses him in his films.

It is all in vain however.

Hulot becomes the protagonist of Tati's life.

CHAPTER 4

On the Beach

> "How do you say *drugstore* in French?"
> *Playtime*

1

Tati often said that dialogue was of little importance, that dialogue was not necessary to understanding his films. Hitchcock said the same thing. In fact, one can follow a Hitchcock film with the sound switched off. Does this absence of dialogue make the film any less cinematographic?

In most of Tati's films, except for *Mon Oncle*, dialogue does not have an immediate narrative function. In many respects, *Mon Oncle* is the one film that most faithfully follows the rules of classical filmmaking and for this reason many critics believed that Tati had compromised his vision.

Scenes can be understood quite well without dialogue. Dialogue provides characters with "traits," much like dress or walk does. Dialogue helps define characters. It appears to us like a fragment of direct, concrete reality:

> *"Cette année, je prends mes vacances en juin."* ("This year I'll be taking my holidays in June.")

"Bon, alors, s'il faut penser à la longueur des poissons." ("Oh well, now we've come to speaking of fish by its length.")

"Roger, t'as pas vu les chiens?" ("Roger, did you see the dogs?")

"Tu comprends, il faut qu'il passe dans les rayons." ("You know, how he has to walk down the aisles.")

When taken out of context, such phrases sound strange, banal, or both. The weird thing is that they sound strange within the context of the film as well: these bits and pieces seem to have been fished out from an unknown world.

Some sentences are like remnants of a time long gone, sounds that as children we could not understand. Still we record these phrases on the magnetic tape of our memory and when they finally re-emerge in a film the words sound raw, since they were never fully grasped and digested. They are – if you can forgive the expression – like memory burps.

2

Indeed, Tati rarely places a certain phrase in the tapestry of the film by chance. Its fate is as fragile as the meaning it conveys, much more than if it had been brought about by the necessities of the drama.

In *Playtime*, we hear the following delightful comment spoken casually by an old-fashioned woman at le Salon des Arts Ménagers : *"Je vais vous dire une chose: j'aime l'opérette, et c'est pourquoi j'ai demandé à ma cousine si elle voulait bien m'y accompagner."* ("Let me tell you something: I love musical comedies. That is why I asked my cousin if she wanted to go see one with me.")

This sentence is spoken right after the Koldehoff incident, a scene apparently unrelated to the scene that follows it. We tell ourselves that there surely is a good reason for this sentence to be in this context.

The fact of the matter is that in *Playtime* characters speak sentences in spite of themselves.

Sitting in the theater we the audience can't help but hear them. These erratic words are like hot irons branding us with their sounds.

3

Three quarters of movies being made today, including the best, use theatrical or radiophonic texts. (Let's not forget how much talking pictures owe to radio.) There is a second group of films that use words like writing *(écriture)* – words seem to be written on the fiber of the soundtrack. This is an important trend in French cinema. In the case of Tati, Fellini and Tarkovski, we should speak of a third type of dialogue. Speech, partly intelligible, partly lost, that seems to flow out of people like sweat.

In a Fellini film sentences wrap you up in their abundance, embracing and turning you inside out. In Tarkovsky's films sentences create long rivulets which run over the ground before being absorbed by the earth; words never happen without first printing a part of themselves on the spectator's mind. In Tati's films, sentences glitter and vanish in the sky like little signals.

Very often we hear solo sentences. In a film like *Mon Oncle*, there is little dialogue in the true sense of the word; that is, words exchanged between two people. When dialogue does occur, it sounds more like squabbling. Characters do not listen to one another, and usually the spectator can't really make out what is being said. Tati refuses to use dialogue; dialogue pulls him back to the very thing he wishes to escape: comedy.

Characters often appear in a duel-like confrontation: one is speaking, the other murmuring, moaning, and more often than not, simply unable to shut up.

Tati uses collective speech: impersonal voices that make the audience feel good. We hear these voices at the Saint-Maur market and on the beach. People play, people shout. It is especially obvious in the scenes with the fritter vendor, who sells fried dough sprinkled with sugar, to children. Here, the flood of words is meant to whet our appetites and bring nostalgia to our hearts.

> Et voilà les bons beignets, voilà, regardez les enfants; les bons beignets, voilà les p'tits gars; voyez si c'est bon, tout chauds, tout bouillants; et hop, voilà une autre

couche, voilà un bon beignet, mais oui, on va mettre un peu de sucre, voilà une bonne ration, tiens mon p'tit gars, tiens goûte-moi ça.

("Here have some delicious fritters. Come and have a look, children. Such sweet dough. Come here, boys. Come and have a taste of these delicious fresh and steaming fritters. And hup . . . here we are. Let's add another layer of sugar to these fritters. Now, take a good look at this fantastic dough. A little more sugar, just a sprinkle more. Okay, my child, this one's for you. Come on, try one.")

The delicacy of this scene has nothing to do with the scene where Gérard is served the soft-boiled egg by his obsessive mother whose kitchen resembles a dentist's office. Her nonstop babble is disquieting. Will it ever come to an end?

4

We hear a number of such "memory burps," as we called them earlier: the forced and satirized dialogue that aims at pinning down the emptiness of the words. In *Les Vacances de Monsieur Hulot*, Martine's aunt monopolizes conversation wherever she can, indefatigably detailing the banality of what is right before her eyes.

Oh, quel ravissant spectacle, n'est-ce pas, cher Monsieur? Justement j'admirais la mer : ces rochers, ces petites voiles blanches, tout ça, c'est vraiment joli. Qu'est-ce qu'on aperçoit là-bas, c'est un nageur? Vous

voyez, là-bas, de ce côté? Pour moi, les vacances au bord
de la mer, c'est vraiment très agréable et reposant. Mal-
heureusement il y a trop de vent, on n'est jamais bien
coiffée, n'est-ce pas?

(Oh, isn't it a delightful sight, sir? I was just admiring
the sea: these rocks, these little white sails, everything is
so pretty. What is that over there? It's a swimmer, isn't
it? Do you see him, over there, in that direction? Holidays at the seaside are very pleasant and restful for me.
Unfortunately it is a bit windy today. How difficult to
keep one's hair in place, don't you think?)

All this is heard in undertone, a sonorous block that
is not permitted to come out into the foreground.
The systematic rubbing out of words in *Les
Vacances* gets justified by the fact that people speak
in order to say nothing. Talking becomes redun-
dant. Phrases are thrown at us in bits and pieces,
fragments meant to remind us that perhaps somewhere we can still find a way of talking that "has
something to say." This notion, however, Tati aban-
dons altogether in his subsequent films.

If we go back to *Jour de fête*, we notice that certain scenes are marked out by an overabundance of
talk. The two fairground workers, Marcel and
Roger, use their caustic wit at the expense of the
postman, greatly beyond what the comedy of the
situation demands. Characters are constantly
pulling François's leg. The village people get out of
control, compulsive, boisterous. Even the old lady
with the goat has a quick tongue in her own way.

A kind of verbal incontinence appears here that
Tati, who was gifted at writing dialogue, would later

remedy. In the later films, he reduces speech as much as he can, and replaces it with concise texts, superbly written and analyzed. We are reminded of Flaubert who gave up the inexhaustible eloquence of first work, *La Tentation de Saint-Antoine*, and disciplined himself to using a more formal type of language, when it came to depicting somber events.

5

Anybody who has spent a day in Rimini, that busy Italian seaside resort during the summer when it's flooded by waves of European tourists, understands why so many foreign languages overlap in the films by Fellini, who was born in a town nearby.

Tati's films are like beaches waiting for international, or better, intercontinental tourists.

He has at least one point in common with Fellini: both use a stock of foreign languages. German often turns up in a Fellini film. With Tati it's English.

This choice did not immediately assert itself. In *Jour de fête*, the people of Sainte-Sévère, and principally the postman, speak with an artificial country accent, which some spectators might find comical. Then, suddenly, we are presented a short film-within-a-film in English.

Les Vacances is a polyglot film. English and Spanish phrases abound.

In *Playtime*, the settings are as international as they can get, Tati even creates an American character. Foreign words and accents, notably German, resound at every crossroad. The film title establishes rapidly the internationalization of a world where English reigns as the universal language for communication and business.

Trafic is a film about a journey. It brings Hulot back to the homeland of the filmmaker's mother. (Claire Von Hoof, Tati's mother, was of Dutch descent.) We hear Dutch being spoken throughout the film. The protagonist speaks English and the garage owner also communicates in English with Hulot.

This Babel of speech has the effect of one language neutralizing another. Language takes on a purely contingent identity. Characters move from French to German and from Dutch to English, all in the same sentence, as if speaking the remains of an original, more universal language that has been lost.

6

If Tati puts a relative distance between words and himself, by mixing one language with another and by delivering fragmented dialogue, it is as though he were saying:

> The content of dialogue is not as important as you think. Don't attribute so much importance to dialogue. I'm adding it in just in case something of value were to come out of the loudspeaker.

And so we are shown people arguing in the distance, too far for us to grasp what it is they are arguing about. If a conversation heats up, it soon calms down. Eventually everyone walks into a bar for a drink and makes up. Everybody's talking but their words and sounds get swallowed by the roaring sea.

CHAPTER 5

Distant Bodies

"Vous l'avez peut-être pas vu, mais vous l'avez pas loupé."
("You might not have see him, but he didn't miss you.")

Jour de fête

1

There's a fable-like joke in *Jour de fête* told in thirty seconds.

The postman on a bike is riding along a country road. A man perched at the top of a slope stands looking at the postman. A wasp buzzes by. We don't see the wasp, but we hear its intermittent buzzing: it is as though the wasp were imprisoned in a jar – the stinging sound goes round and round.

This scene is made up of two shots. One shows the postman on the road riding his bicycle, then suddenly waving his arms about like a windmill, brushing the wasp away. Cut. The second shot reveals a voyeur, not the spectator sitting beside you in the theater, but a man in a white shirt.

Always faithful to the subtle rules of humor, Tati puts a person in the foreground. This person is seen from the back, looking at the wasp and the postman from a distance. On the soundtrack the faint buzzing sound gradually becomes louder, until it finds its way up to us.

All of a sudden, the voyeur starts to wave his arms about.

Eventually, the wasp leaves and the buzzing subsides.

Off we go to the postman whose turn it is to struggle with the insect.

First message of the scene: He who sees is no safer than he who is seen.

Second message: The object of your sight (in this case, the wasp) is a sign that travels to and fro between the seer and the seen.

2

What does vision mean for Tati? Distance. It is a magical phenomenon that creates space between human beings. Vision is the distance between bodies.

When Tati shoots in close-up, he does so not only to excite our sense of sight, but especially our sense of smell, and our intuition.

What is sound? The absence of well-defined spaces necessitates sounds that keep what is shown at a distance.

Sound, too, can be used to lift a detail to the foreground.

3

Just for laughs, let's call *protruding cinema* movies whose baggage of dramatic images gets emptied onto the audience. The art of editing in such movies consists of eliminating the distance found between the audience and the screen: the idea here is to force the spectator to drown himself in the eyes of actors. Cars are shot under the best lighting possible, exaggeratedly so, in order to keep the images moving fast. The majority of movies made today fit into this category.

The other type of cinema digs out a particular image and the audience is asked to linger on that detail. This group of films belongs to *protruding anti-cinema*. In this case, editing is never used to seduce the spectator.

Tati's work belongs to the latter group, even if Tati himself clearly had nothing against protuding cinema. He simply chose what form best suited his vision.

4

Normally, when we watch a person walk away, we zoom-in on him mentally. That is, we follow him with our eyes as he moves away, and we stay with him, in spite of the growing distance. We identify with the gestures and there follows a sort of mental proximity.

On the other hand, to see the world like Tati

does, our eyes must stay where they are, not move from where we are at. We have to look at an object – which is not necessarily obvious – from the distance that our bodies and eyes are in respect to the object observed. We have to "disengage" the mental mechanisms that allow us to appreciate an object in motion.

To respect Tati's point-of-view, it even for a second after watching one of his films, a very particular bodily withdrawal is necessary.

A film by Tati does not follow you with its eyes.

5

The most widely used method of editing in classical cinema consists of switching between the character who watches and the object watched (a friend, a landscape, a detail, or any other thing). Hitchcock founded the elements of his cinema on this simple basic principle – known as shot/reverse shot. This process can become terribly complex the moment you add sounds, which usually have nothing to do with the point of view chosen, or the temporal and spatial constraints of a shot.

Tati draws a lesson from his cinematographic experience from making his first full-length film, which later he puts into practice more successfully. The idea is born during *Jour de fête*, but matures with his other films.

Whenever Tati wishes to concentrate on the gaze of a person, he does so by placing a voyeur in the foreground. Seen from the back or in three-quarter profile, this voyeur is made to face the tableau he observes, a part of which is hidden by the voyeur himself. An excellent example of this occurs in the scene in which François is seen watching a documentary film about the U.S. postal service.

Standing on the outside, François is looking through an opening in the tent set up as a cinema hall. Instead of having the usual two-shot close-up of the voyeur's bulging eyes alternating with the spectacle offered on the screen, Tati uses a strange single shot, an extreme three-quarter shot of François' face outlined on the right by what he is watching – the screen in the background.

To have decided on such a shot is certainly not due to a lack of understanding of the usual rules of editing. Tati knows how to shoot a scene in the traditional way when he wishes to, as is the case with the flirting scene between Jeannette and Roger: both are silent, but appear to be talking – "lip-synching" – thanks to the soundtrack from an American film.

This scene proves that Tati can, if he wants to, easily pastiche the shot/reverse shot. The scene unfolds quickly, going from a close-up of Roger to a close-up of Jeannette, and then to a broader shot of the couple. All is framed, directed and spliced legitimately, and according to Hollywood and universal standards.

"This," he seems to be telling us, "is what I could give you if I wanted. But I don't, because I don't want to."

This stylistic bias, along with Tati's systematic use of the long shot, prevents us from identifying with a character, as we would normally do in a traditional movie. With Tati, it has more to do with our identifying not with an object or person, but with a "particular way of seeing" things.

In *Jour de fête*, Tati takes certain precautions in order to introduce us to his own point of view. He brings one of two characters to the level of form.

In one case, we have the old woman, bent over with age, accompanied by a goat, who comments in her country brogue on the village spectacle. Her "gossip's inner voice" is coupled to her face once only, when she first appears to us. Usually, if she is looking straight at the spectator, she speaks little or not at all. She is normally only allowed to speak when she has her back to us, or in voice over. This old woman is on our side, the spectators' side; with her tittle-tattle she points out things we should be paying attention to, or else introduces new ways of seeing things.

In the second case we have the vehicle-character. Here, it is the young painter who awkwardly sketches village life as he witnesses it. He sketches the villagers while he stands in the square or sits near the fountain, while he limps across the street or hides deep in the café where the good village people retire and get plastered. His likeable smile, however, doesn't stop him from distancing himself somewhat condescendingly from what he sees. Or maybe he himself is getting in the way? The painter excludes himself from the scene – its derision – that he is watching and, because of that, seems to be embarrassed.

After *Jour de fête*, Tati does not resort to this kind of intermediary device again, preferring instead what I would could call "circulating suspicion." People are often suspicious of one another in *Les Vacances* and *Mon Oncle;* glances travel rapidly among people.

What remains constant is Tati's use of the voyeur. Normally seen in long shot and observed in frontal view or profile, the voyeur has the flabbergasted expression of someone in a trance-like state, like the overweight sweeper at the airport in *Playtime* or the young lymphatic painter in *Trafic*. This technical gadget is in line with Tati's refusal of the close-up – the kind of shot he finally gives in to only in *Parade,* and only because it was filmed in video.

What is the difference between the shots in Tati's films and those cut-away shots in other films, in which we are shown the horrified, amazed, ironic expression on the face of a character in close-up we are meant to identify with?

Traditional "cut-aways" isolate the witness-character in a scene and force him to have a reaction by presenting this face as a temporary model of identification. Tati, however, includes a witness in the shot and places him between what is shown and where we the spectators find ourselves. The witness enjoys this space, for he stands in the best position possible to savor the cream of what cinema can offer *en piqué* and in its depth of field.

6

In all his work, Tati uses film's maximum power of
definition to depict exterior as well as interior settings. If he has not succumbed to the traps of
retouched postcards and industrial photographs, he
owes this not only to the beauty and the accuracy of
his camera work, but also, from *Mon Oncle*
onward, to his carefully studied compositions. Principally in his more urban-set films, such as *Mon
Oncle* and *Playtime*, the aesthetic of his images is
often similar to that of images found in commercial
brochures.

Tati's sense of precision comes from a grand
sense of knowing what, sometimes, must be peopled with minute details and what, other times,
must be stripped down to a single person in an
empty scene. No blur is permitted in the image
itself. If there is any sort of blur, it is our perception
of things that is at fault and nothing else. "It is not
me," says the image, "who hides, erases, blurs, or
distorts things, but you."

There is jubilation whenever someone realizes
that perception – his own or another's – is what
alters an object, and that the object itself has not
changed. A person must take this idea of change
into consideration if he is to achieve his real aim.

We find an example of this in *Jour de fête*. A
man with the moustache and a squint (an obvious
homage to Ben Turpin) repeatedly strikes his ham-
mer to the right of the stake he must knock in.
François the postman is clever enough to put a sec-

ond stake to the left of the first one, and in so doing makes the man with the squint believe that the stake he is hitting is the one he wanted to hit all along.

In *Trafic*, Maria's glasses are spattered with ink. She sees dirt blots everywhere on the vehicle the men are washing. When she notices what the real problem is, she smiles and uses the aberration in her own favor, playing with the workers by pointing to spots she knows do not exist. This scene reveals for the first time the playful side of her character, she who seemed so businesslike is on her way to becoming more humane.

This leads us straight to the exquisite formula film critic André Bazin came up with when he tried to define how soundtracks work in Tati's films: "Destroy clarity with clarity." The definition works so well that we could also use it to describe Tati's visual conception of the world.

There is use for neither aberration, nor distortion. Telephoto lenses that squash perspective are to be avoided. (Long focal shots appear only in *Trafic* and, predominantly, in *Parade*.) The wide angle lens exaggerates everything in front you, so stay away from it. The editing must neither stretch out the duration of the shots, nor contract them. Technique must not interfere with the objects filmed. Technique is valid only if it helps capture reality.

Whenever Tati can, he reconstructs objects entirely. He builds Villa Arpel or *Playtime* City from scratch, so he can control every detail of this world.

7

We know that Tati could have shot his films, at least all the full-length ones, in color. *Jour de fête* was shot with color film using a new process called Thomsomchrome, reputed to be of excellent quality. If the film exists as we know it, it is because this process proved to be unusable. Tati was forced to print black and white copies. (After the publication of this book in French, copies containing portions in color were released [Author's note]). Consequently, when we watch *Jour de fête*, we can see where the film was conceived in color, even though some of its effects have been lost. For the screening of the re-release of the film at the Olympia in 1961, Tati had details of certain scenes tinted with a stencil, using a technique called Scopochrome.

Tinting differs from the color image planned at the onset, yet colors details against a black and white surface – the reflector of a bike at night, the banner of a merry-go-round, the three colors of the flag, a glass of cognac, a yellow balloon – end up being quite poetic. (When the balloon bursts or the cognac is downed in one gulp, the vivid colored stain is reabsorbed like an apparition.) The only fault with this process is that it alters the initial definition and simplicity of the images; undergoing an additional generation has its side-effects.

If *Les Vacances* is in black and white, this is due to insufficient funds. Tati wanted to make the film in color. He wished to draw a few laughs by comparing the different qualities of the suntans of the vacationers.

In these two black and white films – the first despite itself, the second because nothing else was possible – it can hardly be said that Tati tries to imitate chiaroscuro. Tati practices a total "high key" style, as is often the case, for that matter, in all comedy.

With his first color film, *Mon Oncle*, Tati throws himself into gaudy electric yellows and reds, blues and greens in the extra-modern settings, and softer hues in the suburb of Saint-Maur. He was later to regret these excesses, and so shot *Playtime* in the opposite way, that is, in the spirit of his re-coloring of *Jour de fête*.

For *Playtime* he works on the spot, during the shooting, as he is conceiving the sets and costumes. He spreads color patches here and there as lifesigns in a dull universe.

The color in *Playtime* participates in the general cleaning-out-by-emptiness operation that is the essence of the film. Before unravelling lifesigns, Tati must weed out the atmosphere and settings of the film.

What is in fact blurred in the generous colors of *Mon Oncle*? The sign and the line.

Filmed largely in real life scenery and on the road with less means than the preceding films, Tati is unable with *Trafic* to manipulate the use of color in as rigid a manner as he did with the studio productions of *Playtime* and *Mon Oncle*. At least he tries to make the Altra lorry (the camping car firm where Hulot works) stand out by painting it a vivid yellow. The car becomes very much a patch of color, an obvious sign against the green of the landscape, glittering beneath the blaring intermittent northern sun. This film mixes images of average quality. Tati shot scenes in the large exhibition hall and traffic-jams with a "candid camera," directing and framing them as best he could. The resulting composite aspect is certainly responsible for the relaxed charm of this praiseworthy film.

8

One might suppose that the distance Tati established between his characters and the audience would be encouraged among the characters themselves. Though bodily contact is rare – this sort of contact appears quite frequently in burlesque works – it is never entirely absent. In Tati's films there are boys in gangs who fight, men who embrace each other, and couples who lose themselves in an embrace. Nevertheless, the camera keeps at a distance until *Parade*.

Tati has a tendency to film in long shot, a style he adopted quite early in his career. The Tati long shot goes through important changes however, as demonstrated in the way he places his camera.

In *Jour de fête*, the camera generally stands at a distance. Tati avoids the close-up, except in the pastiche scene between Roger and Jeannette, yet he refuses to fix these stylistic tics into any particular rule.

In *Les Vacances*, distance is exploited more systematically. The long shot becomes principle; as a consequence, the film seems visually more unified.

In *Mon Oncle*, the camera is clearly closer. Already the limited number of characters (which swarmed in the hotel and on the beach scenes in *Les Vacances*) and the bareness of the scenery (very rich in the preceding film) lead him to simplify his shots. As long as the characters remain the same size in the images, they always seem closer. The close-up is no longer an exception.

In *Playtime*, thanks to the large 70-mm image format with its emphasis on detail, Tati draws away and systematizes the long shot. Almost all his characters are automatically seen full-length.

In *Trafic*, the editing starts fleetingly with close-ups. Tati more willingly shoots the body in close-up, especially in the sequences taken with a candid zoom camera.

With *Parade,* Tati explores the long-focal lens. He frames his subject in distant close-ups (we feel the distance, due mostly to the crushed perspective brought about by the telephoto lens). For the first time the screen is filled with human eyes and expressions. To accomplish this, Tati does what he did in *Trafic*: he films people with a candid camera.

9

It is in *Parade* that we consequently find *in extremis* Tati's first close-ups: a little girl and a little boy in the crowd, their faces round as balloons. This film reveals best the filmmaker's true personality. Here at last is the face that had been more or less hidden by grimaces and a moustache (François) or by pipe and hat (Hulot).

For the very first time we are able to see Tati's characteristic front teeth (those singular upper teeth which from the start he avoided filming) and the expression of his facial expressions during mime numbers. Up till the Hulot films, Tati stays away from the camera, keeping his face blurred and expressionless. The same is true of his voice: he either disguises it (as with the postman) or "unplugs" it from *Les Vacances* onward.

Hulot's notorious silence is not the mime's natural state. For Tati, it is a conquest, a chosen constraint. Speech in his films, as I have remarked, could have flowed quite spontaneously.

Tati chooses, however, to make Hulot, in spite of his silenced voice, an extremely talkative character. We notice this in his behavior, gestures, and even in his immobility. Hulot is constantly correcting his actions, coming back to what he had strayed from. Sitting, saying nothing (in Mme Février's office or in the waiting room of Giffard's company), Hulot is dreadfully present; he is unable to melt into the setting. What does a tall person dream of? To blend into the setting.

Tati gives Hulot some of the postman's unhealthy agitation. His anxiety makes café-owner Bondy, who does not like him at all, say: "That one, when he calms down . . ."

In fact, the protagonist speaks quite a bit in *Jour de fête*, so much so that when nobody is there to listen to him, he goes on by himself. At times, we can make out a second voice behind the postman's conventional country accent and grumbling, at once serious, light, intimate: the director's voice. (*"Il avait une façon unique de commencer une phrase à voix basse,"* remarked Serge Darney, who met Tati shortly before his death ("Hommage à Tati," reprinted in *Ciné-journal*, Paris: Cahiers du cinéma, 1986, p. 133.)

We will have to wait for *Parade* at the end of his career before we hear Tati's singular voice again, as Monsieur Loyal, and in imitating a sports commentator. Tati's voice is captivating: it eliminates any distance that might exist between the actor and the spectator.

Why does Tati refrain from speaking after *Jour de fête*? Perhaps he thought his voice was too enveloping, too absorbing, too beguiling, which would have radically contradicted what he was trying to achieve with his films.

The purpose of distance is to guard against an excessive, disordered proximity.

Order: to channel a generous, chaotic invention.

Reserve: to dam up the muddy flow of feelings.

Tati is all this.

CHAPTER 6

This House Has Eyes

"Je vais te faire visiter mon home."
("Come, I want you to see my home.")
Playtime

1

In his very pertinent analysis of the close-up and long shot, Pascal Bonitzer stresses the fact that these devices work best when put in relation to the human scale. With this in mind, Bonitzer quotes a famous observation by Einsenstein, according to whom "the rules of cinematographic perspective are such that a cockroach filmed in close-up seems more fearsome on the screen than a hundred elephants taken in a long shot."

Let's point out that in the English language a distinction is made between a close image of a face (close-up) and the detail of an object or a part of the body (insert). This distinction does not exist in French; both concepts merge in a single word.

If we use the term "close-up" when referring to a house in a Tati film, and say that it is a key image of his cinematography, the reader is kindly asked to remember that by this we do not mean the detail of a latch or a window, but the whole house seen as a human face.

No one can deny the fact that the Arpel house has eyes: two oval windows in the upper bedroom. (The garage's new door has similar eyes.) With these Tati creates one of the film's most well-known gags. Hulot has come to mend the damaged branches of the espalier, but ends up waking his sister and her husband. Monsieur and Madame Arpel both appear at their respective lit windows and move their heads in such unison that they evoke the pupils of eyes turning in their orbits. The house watches the events, yet somehow is unable to explain what it is that it has witnessed. What we have here is a tight close-up of eyes looking – the only close-up Tati uses before *Parade*.

A foreshadowing of this image can already be found fleetingly in *Jour de fête* – in the scene of the drunk postman doing his nocturnal round – and more directly in *Les Vacances*, where the hotel windows light up at night as we hear the sounds of a boisterous party every time Hulot drives back to the hotel in his noisy jalopy.

A similar event occurs in *Trafic* with Peter's parents' house. Here, Hulot finds himself as if crucified, head downwards, among the ivy that covers the house like hair. The one-eyed face emits a shrew's voice, the first of many angry women to be seen in a Tati film.

This giant face has just witnessed Peter flirting with Maria – the couple Hulot is also looking at. In this scene the house can be said to be owl-like: the image is reinforced by the cry of an owl heard on the soundtrack.

In such cases, the "close-ups" of houses under-
line the presence of a motherly or fatherly couple.
(It is interesting to note that Peter is the same age as
Gérard is during the making of *Trafic*.)

We have already seen a daytime version of this
gag in *Mon Oncle*. The Arpels are standing behind
the oval windows looking at their female neighbor,
for whom Madame Arpel is preparing a scheme of
introduction to Hulot.

Another close-up of eyes is depicted later. This
happens when the Arpels return from the restaurant
and the car lights sweep over the broken plant.
Giant eyes appear on the screen which, without the
Arpels uttering a word, reveal disappointment as
their car backs up and pours light over the damage
done.

This close-up of eyes "which were not meant to
see" is clearly associated in both cases with a blunder (a *bêtise*). The fact that these things become
"eyes that see" and that there is no mention of the
act of seeing conceals a most terrible truth. Something is presented which cannot be erased.

2

Women reign over their homes. In *Mon Oncle*, a
female housekeeper watches the comings and
goings in the building of Old Saint-Maur. Madame
Arpel the housewife sets the overall tone in the
ultra-modern home; she makes all the decisions; she
opens the electric entrance door. Her presence is
felt everywhere in the villa – as she walks, cooks, or

vacuums. All the exasperated husband can emit is a weak plaintive cry; he is silenced by the tinkling of his teaspoon against the coffee cup.

In *Les Vacances*, we very quickly learn who – between a drowsy, bearded husband and an active, inquisitive woman – is the authority figure in the household of Martine's aunt. When Giffard – the walking employee who curtly keeps Hulot waiting in *Playtime* – returns home, he changes the stiff, official bearing he affects at work and becomes a house pet clearly under the control of the matriarchal figure. When the drunken old man in *Trafic* is brought back home by Hulot, he is welcomed by the commanding voice of a wife who will not be told what to do.

3

Tati's two protagonists are not only bachelors (which is common in the movies), but homeless as well.

In *Jour de fête,* we are never shown where François the postman lives. What we are shown is his cloakroom at work. After the events at the fair have taken place, François, now drunk, is seen crawling towards a train. He slides open the door of a goods-wagon and collapses inside. When he awakes, he pokes his nose outside and is completely astonished to find that the wagon has moved. Like many Tati characters, François is a "displaced person" in the literal sense of the word.

In *Les Vacances,* Hulot stays at a hotel. Nothing else is said of his residence or the kind of job he has. Although we are, from time to time, shown Hulot popping his head out of the window in the attic, we are never allowed into his room. Tati is fond of these tiny dwelling places – an attic room, a kitchenette, a motor-home – where we are never invited in. This is true of *Mon Oncle* as well. This is the first time Hulot is given a home, the top floor of a surburban house. *Mon Oncle* is indeed a central film in the Hulotian saga, for it is here that Tati tries to establish roots for his nomadic hero.

Playtime goes in the opposite direction. When Tati pushes his character into a crowd of "near-doubles" and "fake-Hulots," he is in fact depriving his protagonist of any anchorage. At the beginning of the film, Hulot gets off the 73-bus, and at the end Hulot loses himself at the entrance of a supermarket. Hulot does not return home, a home which, less than ever, seems to exist. Nor are there indications that Hulot has a job or even an aim, apart from his mysterious appointment with Giffard, the failure of which does not disturb him in the least. He is an absolute idler.

In *Trafic,* Hulot is integrated, he works as a designer. As he is travelling, he still spends nights out though we are never shown exactly where.

Night is a mysterious elision.

Though the film's plot unfolds mainly on the road, the theme is the car that we are never permitted to enter. First, the narrowness of space in a truck or car and the nearness of actors' bodies force

Tati to use close-ups, which he avoids as much as possible. Second, if Tati were to use close-ups, he would lose what interests him most: voyeurism. In this film especially, if one finds an abundance of close-ups, they are usually filmed with a "candid camera." Car drivers are not aware of being seen and so behave as if in the privacy of their bedrooms: they yawn, pick their noses . . .

Whenever we are shown the interior of a house, the house is usually depicted as a windmill flooded with light. In Martine's aunt's villa of *Les Vacances*, Hulot manages to walk right through the house; in one bound he goes in one door and out the other! The Arpel house in *Mon Oncle,* set on the ground floor, reminds us of a house in a *Salon de l'habitat moderne.* (Tati keeps the rooms on the top floor secret, fiercely concealed from the spectators.) The garage owner in *Trafic* has a glass-walled house. Schneider's apartment in *Playtime* is seen one section at a time. And then there are the faultless Dutch houses whose interiors display themselves like shop-windows, open to the glances of passersby?

The main feature in Tati's films is that public and private realms are inverted. What is private seems to be scattered in front of everyone. On the beach people reveal their intimacy, their skin; they live their family life in open air, in full view of everyone. At the exhibition hall domestic life equipment (floors, electric lights, household appliances, working tables, dust bins) are spread out in one large area for all to see. (What does poor Reinhart complain about, if it is not that the intimacy of his stand, the public place par excellence, has been violated?)

The Altra motor-home is filled with house gadgets. Instead of being brought on time to the *Salon de l'Auto* where it could reveal its intimate details, it ends up being unveiled at the Franco-Belgian border before a horde of customs-officers. There, the female press attaché of the firm, responsible for the camping car, lies down on the vehicle, beside a policeman, without any sort of inhibition as she describes the couchette.

The Arpel house in *Mon Oncle* is like a factory. Garnished with noisy, push-button machines, it is designed after a Plastac model. Madame Arpel shows off her home to friends, just as Monsieur Arpel shows off his factory to visiting businessmen. Yet we are allowed to see moments of privacy at Plastac, which is after all a public and professional building.

In her office, Madame Février, the head of personnel, behaves as if she were receiving people at home. A small clock hammers its bizarre tick-tock and the office communicates with the adjoining washroom through an oval window. We see her straightening out her dress.

Compared with what we might expect from such a bashful filmmaker, the scenes showing feminine intimacy, without being numerous or long, often punctuate Tati's films with indiscretion. The young girl in *Les Vacances* sits at her table in front of her mirror and files her nails. Ostensibly, this is simply a cutaway introduced to justify the fact that

Hulot is being kept waiting before he again performs more blunders at the Arpel home.

But is this really a cutaway?

CHAPTER 7

Just You Wait and See

"Oh, tu n'as rien compris, moi, je t'attendais au
Quick. J'étais là à six heures."
("You don't get it, do you? I have been waiting at
the Quick since six o'clock.")

Playtime

1

At first sight, Tati's films tell the story of a child who
never comes to life. A man and a woman, though
they come close, never meet. Yet meeting places
abound: public waiting-rooms, restaurants, fancy-
dress balls, a fairground, an exhibition hall, the circus. These are public places where men and women
normally pair off – so that a boy or girl may be
born. Such are the kinds of spaces offered young
Barbara, who might very well meet a mature Hulot,
albeit for a fleeting moment. No child, however,
will come from this.

Maybe one is born by fluke.

Eventually something does happen. Someone
ends up going away, profoundly moved, possibly
pregnant, ready to love. But that kind of ending
won't happen just yet – it's not what we are shown.

Maybe the clean May air in *Playtime* is meant

to convey a different sort of symbol – these sounds, fragrances at last breathable, might very well be the pollen of fecundity!

2

With *Playtime* Tati manages to build new sets with what *Mon Oncle* leaves us. We are asked to re-deal the cards and to tidy up. There are no more irresponsible mixtures. ("Today," Tati complains, "people mix everything together.")

On one side, female tourists in a package tour arrive from distant America; the herd is preceded by twin nuns. The twenty-five ladies are counted and recounted, sorted, divided, and re-organized by their masculine guide. On the other side, the men follow, channelled into groups and guided by hostesses. They either work in Tati-Ville or have come here on a business trip.

Playtime orchestrates this separation of sexes: on one side female tourists; on the other, businessmen. This peaceful movement is regulated by the voices of guides and dispatchers resounding out of loudspeakers.

At Orly airport, a lady in a fur coat and an important gentleman in an overcoat emerge from separate worlds.

It is this sorting out of things that starts up the centrifugal force of the film. There is no mixing of things, especially not the sexes. This is the backdrop to the evening's dance that awaits the couples crowding the hall.

Tati's last work, *Parade*, is set at the circus. A little boy and girl are accompanied by their parents: the father for one, the mother for the other. The eternal separation of sexes. At the end of the film the boy and girl meet, only after they have sniffed one another like puppies.

3

Parade is a spectacle which refrains from telling any story. The meeting of the two children is constantly interrupted by cutaways to the general public.

On the left, a perfect little girl in a blue dress claps her hands at everything. Sweet, alluring, conformist, she behaves well. On the right, the little blonde-haired boy in a cowboy outfit is obviously bored. Once the show is over, the little man and the little woman stand in the ring of the empty circus. Their games monopolize the screen, which until then had been peopled by artists and spectators.

We mustn't exaggerate the significance of this encounter though. Here are two children playing together but for an instant. At times the girl stops to admire the boy, especially when he rides a donkey or plays the horn. He, for his part, doesn't even give the girl a single glance.

When the children leave the circus, the camera lifts its gaze to the ceiling and everything comes to an end. The camera catches the two parents in the empty rows in the back of the circus. The fair-haired man and the shy brunette have stayed for

their children. Neither looks nor speaks to each
other, even though they are close to one another,
alone in the enormous space.

Like other spectators, they have witnessed a
strange experience – a sort of fertilization under a
microscope. Everyone hoped to see nature "come
alive."

Using the powerful recording capacity of video,
Tati gives the children total freedom. He does not
even pass on any sort of acting instructions. He
gambles: he places one vis-à-vis the other. All is
present, but nothing happens once again.

4

Tati's films actually tell stories of avoidance. Hulot's
apartment in *Mon Oncle* lies at the top of a delight-
fully complicated house, in shape and access. It has
a labyrinth-staircase which, when going up and
back down again, prevents Hulot, gentleman that
he is, from the meeting the alluring female neighbor
wearing only a slip.

Les Vacances and *Playtime* follow a pattern
based on the same principle, which is as easy to con-
ceive as it is difficult to carry out. Take a man and a
woman, and set them free on their respective paths
in this maze-garden. In both films, there are scenes
with Hulot alone and scenes where he is alone with
the young woman. And then there are scenes with
points of contact between the two, though not necessarily depicting the two face to face.

In *Playtime,* Hulot is never less "with" Barbara

than precisely when he is with her dancing at the Royal Garden. Yes, Barbara is willing. When she is shown in her hotel bedroom, bathed and getting ready for the evening, she puts on a happy face, as though she were about to get married. "*Comme vous allez être belle,*" an old chambermaid says to her in admiration. Here is a young woman about to participate in an important ritual.

Then, as in *Les Vacances*, the woman hears a noise that makes her go to the window (a backfiring car): it is Hulot driving by.

In *Playtime*, Barbara is suprised by the sound of a whistle coming from a voluble Parisian policeman in the street (like a morse code: *ta-ti–ti-ti-ta*). But she has not seen him yet. Not far away, Hulot is locked in the Salon des Arts Ménagers; he too hears the whistle. He goes onto a terrace, from where he can look into the distance. Without Barbara or Hulot noticing one another, the whistle acts like a signal they both receive, a secret sound which unites them for a while.

5

The point is to let oneself be carried away by life and become a go-between with uncertain intentions. This Hulot does in theory. And so do Tati's attractive, quiet women: Martine in *Les Vacances* and Barbara in *Playtime*.

Take note, however: Tati creates opportunities for the union of men and women in which nothing happens.

In *Mon Oncle*, nothing happens during the big garden-party organized by Hulot's sister to marry him off; nor does anything occur, once again, in the most developed and most complex scene Tati has ever written: the dance at the Royal Garden. (The plot of one of his first short films, *Gai dimanche*, revolves around a picnic turned disastrous. There are a good number of trouble scenes in the hotel dining-room of *Les Vacances* too. In *Mon Oncle*, Madame Arpel's kitchen, as well, with all its gadgets, becomes a centre of activity.)

The Royal Garden. Women are led there in a herd, a real female cargo delivered to Hulot. Black musicians lead the clientele into a Dionysian dance.

The atmosphere of sexual tension prevails at the party in *Mon Oncle* as well: the shrill laugh of Pichard's wife, the provocative tight trousers of Walter's girlfriend, Hulot's saucy stories, the ulterior motive of this meeting.

Such an atmosphere is reinforced by nature itself (heavily aquatic) and the incidents which disrupt the calm. If trouble is encountered again, it is sublimated, diluted into a collective good humor and camaraderie which cut short any eroticism. The context itself – the promiscuity, the deeply low-necked dresses of the women, sweating bodies due to a malfunction in the air conditioning – gets rather "hot." The heat arising from this scene carries us into a strange kind of abstract, disembodied climax.

We find a touch of direct, nearly sadistic sexuality in the detail: the women's backs are branded by the chairs with an "iron" crown motif. These signs stress the fact that the bare shoulders and backs of beautiful women possess erotic charm.

Perhaps too much so.

Whatever nakedness and tempting skin are shown in *Les Vacances* (whose plot is ideal for showing a lot of skin!) can be reduced to the bare back of the young female lead: on the beach, at the bathing hut changing and, later, at the fancy-dress ball wearing a Colombine dress with a low neckline.

Hulot's hand will inadvertently slide down the slope of this woman's back – a gag indicative of how far he is from being the asexual being he pretends to be. What should he do, he who can dance so well?

In *Playtime*, Tati won't stop things from happening, such as preventing Hulot from meeting Barbara. He has them cross paths several times, unknowingly, inside the club. First, Barbara is judged on her arrival by the staring clients already at the Royal Garden: "What is she doing here? She's too young to be with those older ladies in hats." In spite of Hulot's stubborn refusal to being dragged along by his determined friend, he ends up beside Barbara.

If the door smashes to pieces, it is to a large extent Hulot's fault. But isn't Barbara, who is standing on the other side of the door, also to blame? This connection has to be decided by the spectator, for the film will never weave cause and effect together, not even symbolically.

When Hulot and Barbara dance together, Tati

leaves them alone, as if to say: "This is the private life of my characters, it's not for you to see."

In the script published in number 199 of *Cahiers du cinéma*, there figures an unedited scene with Hulot and Barbara dancing, and Schneider's teenage daughter at the dance too, having come without her parents' permission.

Where has this scene gone? Vanished.

Yes, no doubt, it has flown away into the sky.

6

Everything happens, it seems, *a contrario*.

In *Trafic*, Maria is responsible for an accident. No one gets hurt – only the vehicles do. Men and women check to see if their arms and legs are still there, if they can move their limbs. They then spread out into the woods and gather the parts of their cars strewn about like the limbs that could have come from their own bodies.

Suddenly a little car arrives at a slow pace, zig-zags, and topples into the ditch well before it reaches the scene of the accident! The driver, an old Dutch-man soaked up to the gills with alcohol, is injured: he is holding his leg.

The succession of these two events is purely fortuitous. The film leaves the spectator the responsibility of interpreting these shots as he or she likes.

One of the consequences of this accident is that Maria meets the old man's son who soon tries to seduce her.

Maria fends him off.

Hulot drives the older man back home to his wife, and finds himself involuntarily in the midst of a threesome – maybe the only one of its kind in Tati's work.

If there is any ambiguity in these scenes, it is mostly due to the idea that nothing is broken *("rien de cassé")*.

In the first part of *Playtime*, Giffard tries to catch up with Hulot, with whom he has an appointment in the morning. Unfortunately, he will violently bump his nose on a glass door he has not seen.

"It's nothing, it's nothing," he moans as he holds his nose, impotent in his anger.

That *rien* will, however, become a momento – a bandage on his nose – that Giffard will carry late into the evening.

In the second half of the film, Hulot gets hurled out of the club by his doorman friend. On his way out he bumps into the glass door, which yields and shatters into a thousand pieces. Hulot comes out of this accident unscathed, but the spectator is left wondering whether or not this luck is the result of Hulot having become "immune," thanks to Giffard's bad luck.

This is how a film by Tati works. An accident occurs, leaving its victims covered with wounds. And like the ripples of waves, each one of these injuries is then transferred from one person to another.

7

Martine appears outside the bathing hut, clearly naked under the towel she has wrapped around her body. Hulot happens to be passing by and notices her. Martine jumps back into the hut. At this very moment Hulot sees fat Schmutz lean towards a small opening in the door of the hut. Hulot kicks chivalrously Schmutz in the rear.

The spectator quickly learns that if Schmutz is leaning forward it is to take a picture of his family standing behind the hut where Martine is hiding. Seen from Hulot's point of view, however, space being compressed, Schmutz has become a voyeur.

Schmutz rapidly turns around, not fast enough to see who his fleeing assailant is.

In the background, Hulot stands chatting with Martine's aunt.

Cut to Schmutz again, and then back to Hulot, who is cowardly running away. Martine's aunt is left prattling to herself.

Schmutz notices a boy nearby and suspects him. The innocent boy doesn't understand why he is the target of such a dirty look and takes refuge in a bathing hut. Schmutz moves towards the boy, this time actually taking up the voyeur's position, from which Hulot believed he had seen him in in the first place. End of scene.

Film critic Barthélémy Amengual writes that "the incident is closed" for the spectator; no follow-up to the scene is given.

If we analyse this sketch out of context, it is typical of Tati's micro-scenarios. Actions vanish in thin air, without a trace, leaving the spectator with a sense of uneasiness. The image of Schmutz accusing an innocent boy remains engraved in our conscious.

A man suspects another man, who is the wrong man. Suspicion leads one to look at the other with undefinable scrutiny. Men, in Tati, have a thousand reasons to look at each other.

8

Tati tells a story:

> One day I saw a very serious gentleman going to a board of directors' meeting. As he locked the car, his tie got caught in the door. There he was: imprisoned outside his car, hanging from a locked door, keys in hand, but, from where he was, unable to reach the lock (*Cahiers du cinéma*, No. 483, May 1958, p. 7).

Tati goes on to say that this sort of "natural gag" could easily develop into something fascinating. Had he continued the gag by telling us the outcome of the scene he would have killed the humor. It is best to leave the spectator to his imagination.

> So here we have a gentleman, whose tie is caught in his car door, his keys, and the unreachable doorlock. That's all that has happened to him. One could continue to exploit the situation: one could have this gentleman's wife pass by and surprise him in the company of a young girl who had come to help him . . . On the pretext that "it is only a movie," we are often asked to con-

tinue, continue . . . But not at all! What makes this scene
funny is precisely the fact that it stops where it stops.

Many good films exploit the love triangle. Tati has
never made films about rivalry, even though he
often alludes to rivalry.

In *Jour de fête* we have one such scene. It happens when the fairground people come to present a
Western to the village people. Its title appears on a
poster: *The Arizona Rivals.*

Unlike the documentary on the postal service,
we do not get to see anything of this film. Nobody
in the village whispers a word about it. During the
projection test in the village square, however, we
are given a taste of what to expect.

The dialogue in English is heard when Jeannette, the village girl, and Roger, the fairground
worker, exchange glances. The words from the
Western voice the emotions Jeannette and Roger
dare not speak; all they do is mime the postures.
When the lines are spoken in voice-over by the
American actor ("Daphne, I love you"), Roger
silently acts the part of the cowboy, holding his tool
like a colt. When the actress replies, "Oh Ji!," Jeannette turns her eyes down and bashfully smiles.
Both are faithful to the dialogue, identifying silently with the characters in the Western. They speak to
each other using the lines they hear coming from
the loudspeaker in the square. In so doing, they
mimic a love that will never fully realize itself.

This "love scene" enables Tati to quote visually,
via sound and image, traditional editing. Never
again will Tati use this type of editing: going from

the shot of the man to another of the woman in a single scene, and lastly cutting to the rival. For Jeannette has a rival, and a tough one at that: Roger's wife.

Rivalry is a theme Tati returns to in the most convoluted of situations. Hulot flees from rivalry, but eventually it catches up with him. As soon as he gets the chance to declare his love, a rival turns up. When someone "seduces" Martine in *Les Vacances* or the housekeeper's girl in *Mon Oncle*, Hulot gives in and quietly disappears. (The only explicit "duel" Hulot will ever engage in occurs near the end of *Mon Oncle,* when he inadvertently finds himself in the middle of a fist fight in front of a café at night.)

Rivalry does reappear, however, in the most unexpected way. As Madame Arpel keeps bringing up Hulot to her husband, Monsieur Arpel becomes jealous, not of a man who lusts after his wife, but of the good-for-nothing brother-in-law with whom his son Gérard enjoys himself more.

When Hulot brings home his happy nephew Gérard covered with mud, Monsier Arpel and Hulot come face to face for an instant, standing symmetrically opposed like enemies in a Western. The gag is entirely based on this simple posture: hands on hips, a pose that has different meanings to each man. For one, it is reproach and, for the other, a way of being curious.

This is the attitude Tati gives to his protagonist on the posters for his film. Hulot should have been a cowboy.

As for the Oedipean rivalries, Tati spoils us with

fathers, *padri padroni* types, short plump bosses who are quite harmless and end up by being dear to him.

9

Bosses in Tati-Land are depressed. We find an angry boss in every Tati film. These authority figures have fits of anger towards subordinates or intruders that rapidly change into bickering and complaining: "This is my house, my invention, my work!" These men possess none of the self-assurance invested in them by their social position. They get affected by events and deflate.

These characterization applies equally to the irascible café-owner Bondu in *Jour de fête*, Arpel in *Mon Oncle*, Reinhart (*Playtime*), as well as to the anonymous boss of Altra, forever a prisoner of his own impotency and masochistic temper.

Let's look at the German industrialist who invented the door that won't slam. It is a symbol of course. The inventor should be proud to have designed it, the problem is that when he is angry and wants it to slam violently, the door will not go "bang."

In Tati's films bosses hurt themselves with their own words.

Monsieur Arpel's tirade is worth quoting in full, if only because it is one of the few (and short) tirades we find in Tati's films. It is spoken over images of Hulot quietly slipping off as the shadow of Madame Arpel is seen in the washroom scrubbing down her dirty child). Entirely in voice-over, the voice might have been added afterwards. Still this doesn't weaken its importance. On the contrary.

> Look at this, then! Look at this! Incredible! That's just great! He's gone too far! Honestly, such a nuisance. Oh – no, no, no! If he doesn't like it here . . . very well . . . why doesn't he say so! Really, who built this house? I did, right? The studies, the clothes, who buys them? Me! If anyone wants to take my place? Well! Don't mind me! Go on! Go on then!

How can we not notice with what strange insistence Arpel challenges Hulot "to take his place," a place no one ever disputed. (Even if Hulot inattentively parks his motorbike in the space specially reserved for his brother-in-law's car at Plastac.)

"Admit it, you're jealous," Madame Arpel says to her husband.

Tati's portrait of Hulot's sister is at once affectionate and distant. Clearly, of the two, she is the older, protective sister who dearly loves her brother. When his sister got married, Hulot lost more than he is willing to admit. Perhaps here lies one of Tati's central themes: where is the caring sister in the women of the simple world?

10

François rides his bike on a country road in *Jour de fête*. A wasp (in fact, just a buzzing sound) hovers over him, stretching sound webs all around his bike.

After three sedentary films, *Trafic* takes Tati

back on the road again. Maria is an insect in human form with a skirt! She spins her little yellow sports car around the large Altra truck, not as a coach fly, but as a lorry wasp would do. Forever chattering away, she glides in exasperation over the northern European roads at such a speed that we are never quite sure if she is preceding or following the Altra truck. When she finally causes a pile up, she throws a traffic policeman at a crossroad into total confusion. Maria is a thought flying round and round in our heads, oblivious to the straight lines on her path, forever changing.

There is a subtle "running gag" about the clothes Maria wears throughout *Trafic*. If we pay close attention, we notice that every fashionable suit she slips into ressembles the outfit worn by the worker beside her. Her dungarees rhyme with those of the repairman she drives back in her car. Another outfit is similar to the livery worn by the hotel doorman in front of whom she has come to park.

At one point in *Mon Oncle*, Tati has the neighbor deck herself out with such a ridiculous dress that, from a distance, Madame Arpel mistakes her for a pestering carpet salesperson.

Tati's women are shameless when it comes to clothes. They have a sort of personal ostentatiousness, not in what they reveal, but in what they cover themselves up with. Obviously, Tati is a person who prefers a certain traditional reserve, the kind he endows most of his heroines with. He keeps caricature for his secondary characters.

After reading what has been written above, you

could too quickly accuse Tati the filmmaker of being somewhat of a misogynist. Every type of woman finds her way into his films: the shrew and the missus, the goody-goody and the nympho, the snob and the Lolita. But there is scarcely room for the simple woman.

He who, in his doctor's waiting room or at the hairdresser's, has come across the caricatures by Kiraz, Faizant, or Jean Bellus, published in *Jours de France,* will understand where Tati's sarcastic imagery comes from. These women cackle, shriek, make disgusted faces, express their raptures in the most exaggerated way. These ladies wear extravagant hats and fur coats. When they are standing, they take on affected and obvious poses. We have to wait for *Trafic* –Tati's last trip to Rubens' homeland – before we see women with full, erotic bodies. *Trafic* reconciles Tati to life and the world. Here, bodies and skin grow beyond being silhouettes and attain a third dimension.

In works where the spoken word has such a peculiar status, women who do speak use speech purposefully. If Tati often portrays women who "speak for nothing," or "speak just for the sake of speaking" (like Martine's aunt), he also shows that the only solution for the man in the presence of these motor-mouths is to withdraw into silence and become unhappily submissive. Even in the silent scene showing the Arpels awakening, Madame Arpel manages to tap noise from her slippers and rustle from her cleaning apron. Her non-verbal chatter can be at times stunningly sonorous.

Nevertheless, these women are in fact friendlier and more lively than the reserved, well-educated women in *Jour de fête* (Jeannette), *Les Vacances* (Martine), or *Playtime* (Barbara).

Barbara is charming, yet insignificant to the point where nothing can save her. One might say that she is the film's major fault. Tall as she is (an aspect which is not without importance for Tati), Barbara has nothing in the least suggestive about either her looks or walk. Endowed with a graceful poise, yet without a figure, she is tall and slim, elegant, yet dull, devoid of the magic charm of the younger women coming from Truffaut's good families. The young German au pair playing the role of an American on holiday looks a tad too English. Barbara Dennek is severely international.

Yet we notice what makes her what might be called a "carrier." Barbara possesses the neutral aspects of the Virgin Mary waiting for the Annunciation. A young page, a white goose, she opens herself to the operation of a "marking" so that she can be sent back into the sky as a dove.

11

The unfinished aspects of Hulot which Bazin speaks of, Barthélémy Amengual very appropriately compares to his female non-partners:

> Alone, Monsieur Hulot seems unfinished. In a similar way but to a lesser extent, so is the young blonde (Nathalie Pascaud) who expects to find in others "her

nose. When a thing captures his attention, no part of his face can be said to be the centre of his concentration: not the eyes, not the nostrils, not the forehead. His pipe is an appendage he sticks into his mouth. The hat which conceals part of his head plays a crucial role in hiding his facial expressions. His sense of direction and slanting pose leave us wondering. This faceless person might be a conscious creature, but in reality Hulot is just the extension of the path he walks on.

4

The line, more important than the volume of things and beings, does not enclose volume. Before *Trafic*, objects and bodies are without substance. Look at the line these non-substances draw. Tati's characters are nothing more than silhouettes; even the little plump men seem like roundish shadows. They have no flesh. Flesh spoils the line, adds weight.

François and Hulot have bodies in the shape of a line – a fishing line in wait of sensations. But sensations alone?

What is Hulot searching for? What smells tempt him? Where is he going with such determination?

Perhaps he's heading for language.

François on his bike meanders his way through lines, curves, detours. Yet the letters he carries manage to reach their destinations. The day he follows a straight bee line doesn't promise better results.

Catastrophe lies waiting around the corner. Sure, a letter gets delivered, in spite of the danger a few steps ahead. The person expecting the letter risks not receiving it, because the straight line leads François right into a river.

All François wishes for is to imitate the U.S. postmen he saw in the documentary film. He wants to be like those angel-like men and women who stop at nothing, not even fire.

If a road suddenly comes to a dead end or if water floods the ground, François can always hop on a helicopter or plane.

5

Tati prefers taking the longer path.

Hulot's singular tennis technique comes about by imitating the movement a salesman taught him. It best exemplifies his love for the indirect path. First, he holds the racket like a frying pan. Then he draws the racket abruptly towards his body, before brandishing it vigorously to strike the ball. Hulot never misses a shot.

The neon arrow at the entrance to the Royal Garden is another example of Tati's preference for the longest way. The light coils upon itself in a spiral before going out of the circle, where it then points at a target: the entrance into the restaurant.

The motif used as a logo in *Trafic* is the junction. The straight road leads to another road which curves away into the path destiny forces him to follow.

By dint of cutting across arrows and lines, he often finds himself turning round in circles. This is what happens in the end when all the roads flow into a traffic jam.

What else is there to do, if not to add merry-go-round music to the spectacle? And so the wheel keeps turning round and round.

Should he follow the curving line? Is curve the only path that leads to grace? It is never so simple.

If the stone path in the Arpels' garden seems ridiculous, it is because its loops and curves force people to meander about before they can reach the threshold of the house. Yet the host as well as the visitor follow it faithfully, instead of cutting straight across the lawn.

We laugh at the settings in *Playtime* because they encourage people to turn right when they could very well turn left.

The real question we should ask ourselves is not whether or not the straight line is better than the curve. No, what should concern us is what happens if we do follow the lines, even those in invisible ink, that lie ahead of us.

CHAPTER 9

Tati-World or Juxtaposed Worlds

"Les dix millions de kilomètres carrés ne comportent que des chemins carrossables. Rien n'arrête le postman yankee. Pour lui, là où s'arrête la route, le ciel continue."

("Thousands and thousands of miles for the postman to travel. At the end of road, the sky begins.")

Jour de fête

1

Les Vacances presents itself like a minature ecosystem. A woman picks up with unceasing delight seashells that the shore offers in numbers. She says, *"Oh! a seashell"* and, one by one, passes the shells to her husband who, silently, chucks them back in the sea.

It is in *Mon Oncle,* however, that the idea of an ecological cycle is most present. We can see it throughout the film. In the beginning, a ragman returns to Plastac the waste that he picked from some suburb dustbin. We can assume that these shining plastic pipes were once manufactured at the factory. But metres of pipe prove to be faulty. The discarded plastic is loaded onto a cart and sent back to its maker. The cycle is eventually interrupted, sorry, blocked. Faulty plastic can't be recycled by the small town.

In *Mon Oncle* the modern world maintains its cleanliness by shipping its waste to small town garbage dumps.

An old decrepit suburb is about to be razed. The modern world throws its old-world decay into gaping dustbins. By the end of the film we are left asking ourselves: "How should we get rid of what's left?"

Call Hulot? Let's send him into thin air.

The pipes? Throw them into the sea.

More than in any other Tati film, *Mon Oncle* is filled with references to the dirty and clean: Madame Arpel owns a duster; Gérard dirties himself while playing with his friends. Back home he is ferociously given a shower by his mother.

A dog lifts its hind leg. A second dog jumps over it.

And water, there is plenty of water everywhere. The garden party scene revolves around water which floods the lawn and soaks the guests' feet. Water, high and low, spits out of the fountain-fish in different colors.

The last night, strange and interminable as it seems, represents an enigmatic point in the film. When the plastic pipe is thrown into the river, it splashes near lovers kissing on the river bank.

"A suicide," the woman screams.

"It's blood," the man yells and dives into the river.

When he comes out, he is furious, thinking someone has played a stupid prank on him. He runs after the man in his cart who flees, looking guilty.

There follows a crazy and confusing fight scene which takes place in front of a bistro. Roger pulls off his jacket. So does Hulot and lands his fist on an innocent bystander's cheek.

The fighting, however, is short. The men quickly start laughing and bring the argument to an end by walking into the bar.

Hulot's nephew Gérard is overjoyed to be able to sit in the cart on the driver's seat, pulling the reins of the horse as he waits for his uncle to come out.

In the meantime, Monsieur and Madame Arpel spend a romantic evening together without their son.

The following day in Saint-Maur, we see Hulot leaving his apartment. The housekeeper's daughter is now a beautiful woman whose tip of the nose Hulot suddenly hesitates to touch. Instead – and it is such a sweet twist – he decides to touch the mother's nose.

What has happened? Nothing is said.

Hulot has quietly witnessed the transformation of a little girl who used to spin around him, showing off her new Sunday dress, into a woman. Her body has changed. Her mother has changed as well, she too acts differently.

The plastic "blood" thrown into the river the night before – could it possibly refer back to this young woman's lifeblood?

2

With *Playtime*, Tati pushes off screen not only any direct allusion to sexuality, but also things that could be considered daring, or spiral out of proportion.

This is the first time Tati deliberately confines his universe to what we see on screen. He no longer seems interested by what happens beyond the frame.

A handful of flowers on the vendor's stand acts as a sign of what has vanished forever.

Let's take a look at the restaurant scene. There is enough material here to depict one person's complete life cycle. We have a kitchen, a dining-room, a dustbin – objects that we get a glimpse of in Hitchcock's London as portrayed in *Frenzy*. Nothing of that here.

When we see *Cours du Soir* – that short film Nicolas Ribowski shot on Tati while he was shooting *Playtime* – we are startled to discover what the actual backdrop of *Playtime* looks like.

The city off-screen is a wasteland of broken huts on overgrown weeds. This is the reality the film doesn't show. Yet it is these barren surroundings that give birth to Tati-Ville, born like a mushroom.

Both water and earth appear profusely in *Mon Oncle*: there's the earth from Arpels' garden which Pichard digs to repair the fountain; then there's the earth crammed with rubbish that in places looks like ruins. The commonness of it all strikes us because *Playtime* reveals such a dramatic change of universe.

No more earth or water here, only sky to which our eyes are drawn. Instead of the sexy Lolita of the Suburbs, we have a pristine woman finding her way through the artifical settings of the Salon des Arts Ménagers. Instead of waterworks, canal systems, and pipes, we have air drafts and electricity.

Sexuality is uprooted like a weed. If it were to grow again, it would be in a different, more intellectual and spiritual way.

The music, however, which opens the credits in *Playtime*, the drumming, the frenzy of a dull boom-boom, is the same music we have heard before. It's the call from the gut.

Mon Oncle takes place on the ground floor where we risk getting our feet wet, and this actually happens. Hulot goes to the Arpels' upper floor to wring out his striped socks.

Playtime lifts us up to where water can no longer threaten us: we find ourselves up in the clouds.

3

Tati's skies are not vertical. If the earth is ground level, then the sky is a horizontal plane, a landing, the second storey of life. Earth mixes with water, too much so, allowing water to gush everywhere, sparing nothing, dissolving all lines.

In *Mon Oncle*, there is a map of the world

behind the bosses' desk at S.D.R.C.. Beyond the counter of the travel agency in *Playtime* we discover another map of the world.

First stories and ground levels meet; the road markings are similar.

"At the end of the road, the sky begins."

4

Schmutz is elsewhere. His body might be on the beach, but his mind is in the clouds. He thinks about things going on in other places – the International Stock Exchange perhaps. When the phone rings for him at the hotel, he starts swimming towards the open sea. He is literally rushing towards the place that is calling him.

5

Tati's world is essentially made of air. He lives on the top floor of the apartment building. Does that mean we can find him everywhere?

Air is the pathway for communication, the material that music is made of.

Tati is fond of color, its music as unpretentious as the very substance of air.

We never feel the density of matter in a Tati film: not the thickness of wood, not the hardness of metal, not the roughness of skin. Tati achieves a sense of lightness in the way he frames his images and through his choice of lighting and sounds. The particular attention he gives to sound contributes to the impression of working with weightless and hollow objects.

Sound doesn't transmit the heaviness of a creaking door, the roughness of grating metal, or the suppleness of a shoe. Tati never makes us feel the fullness and consistency of matter. This is exactly the opposite of what happens, for instance, with Robert Bresson. He purposely ascribes the sound of emptiness – the sound the stuff coming out of Plastac makes.

6

The vacationers enjoy a moment of gymnastics on the beach. They inflate their chests and obey the instructor who keeps time with his whistle. The instructor approaches Hulot and offers him advice. In the background, the vacationers continue doing their exercise, keeping their chests inflated like balloons. Nothing is ever lost in this universe.

Later, at a burial ceremony, an old man notices a strange looking funeral wreath: the tube from Hulot's Amilcar wheel that someone heedlessly hung near the coffin. We hear it deflating with a "puff."

In a very concrete way, here is a symbol, a little vulgar maybe, yet quite appropriate in representing a person's last breath. The man breathes deeply, inflating his chest as if to remind himself that he is really alive. Strong and healthy men and women

emit a similar sounding "puff" when they let air out
from their mouths. Very much like a tube mistaken
for a wreath.

What sound is heard is forgotten. There exist
certain sounds which aim at making us forget.
Music, that is, some music, if sublimated, helps us
forget the material characteristics of sound.

However, in a film by Tati, sound insists on making its presence heard. Creatures and objects emit
sounds through little openings; some matter, when
rubbed against matter, produces the voice of espacing
sounds. These "farts" – many sounds in a Tati film
sound like farts – never reveal the volume, mass, or
strength of the bodies that sound them. These are
never more than localized sounds, torn from the
"orifice" of a particular source.

7

During the silent movie era, films were accompanied by sound effects performed live, especially to
punctuate a comic stunt or thunder. Music halls
champion a long tradition of utilizing sound effects.
Here sounds were evidently used more in synchro-
nization (at one with the visuals) than to emphasize
spatial reality. Modern cinema is clearly no different.

What makes the bell on François' bicycle so special? Or the sound of the trumpet rising from
Hulot's Amilcar so unique?

Many have criticized these sounds for being
immobile, for not moving along with their sources.

Precisely, these noises are, first and foremost, placed to be heard in the specific shot where they appear. They must be totally fixed. Tati doesn't even make the slightest attempt to simulate perspective by changing the position of these sounds.

Numerous Tati gags spring directly from this technique of finger-pointing sound effects. While dubbing and adding noises on the soundtrack to his films, Tati would offer his characters the chance to play the role of the sound-effects engineers.

In *Mon Oncle*, a passer-by notices the concierge plucking the feathers of a dead fowl. As a joke, he imitates the cackling the bird would have made had it still been alive. The concierge jumps, afraid she has suddenly brought the bird in her hands back to life.

In the short film, *Gai dimanche* (1935), two gags follow this similar pattern. A boy hides behind a car whose motor is obviously not turned on and imitates the noise of its running engine.

A girl blows a trumpet, the sound of which makes adults turn around expecting to see a chicken.

What do these sounds add to reality?

They lift the real world to another dimension.

A dead chicken comes alive. A car seems about to drive away, even if its motor is turned off.

Our sense of sight has been altered.

We can begin to dream.

8

Tati works assiduously at creating sounds that stick

to one place at a time. He deals with sound, as it were, as though it emerged from the centre "bell" of an object. This is in perfect contradiction with everything that has been said about the infinite possibilities of sound in film and how sound can easily brim over the image.

Tati could not have made a better choice than to take as the symbol for his technique the persistent, piercing, unstable, shifting, and yet immobile ring of the *grelot*. What is a *grelot*? A grelot is a small bell that we hang on something to signal its movement. It produces those high notes we hear in a little seashell. Though muffled, these noises occupy the entire spectrum of our listening. Like the varying frequencies of speech and the transitory slippage of language, these sounds beg agility and attentiveness in hearing, in order that we better catch the direction of sound.

Compare this to the tolling of a normal bell. A sonorous wave spreads out from a central point; a noise that makes the listener forget the substantiality of matter. It limits the spatiality of its cause and origin and becomes a wave that ripples in the sky the same way that falling rocks and the passage of ships create ripples in water.

Tati does not want the sound of such a bell. He hooks sound onto things, restricting sound to the bit of cause and effect it may have. He confines it to a tiny and precise spot.

No sound will by itself disturb the space. Sound in a Tati film is material and materialistic; it doesn't "express" the particular substance of an object.

Sound cracks the world open, reveals the pieces within: matter.

9

Because sound acts as its own onomatopoeia, it has little or no concrete value as the expression of the density of objects. It is more a sign, a substitute for language.

Through its rhythm and articulation, sounds speak of abstract matters. This is why Tati is so fond of detached and defined noise: the tick-tock of a clock or the thud of footsteps, the knocking of a ping-pong ball, the plok of a bouncing ball, the clunk of a closing door. Articulated noise.

In *Trafic*, a predefined sound corresponds to a car passing by. The noise of the traffic does not melt into a continuous hum.

Tati often inscribes a particular sound on the backdrop of continuous human activity: the market at Saint-Maur, children playing, cries on a beach, the commotion of waiters in a restaurant kitchen. Here again, an inversion occurs.

The voices of men and women calling – as well as the sound of animals (fowl, birds, herds of animals) – color this world. Uninterrupted hubbub reverberates in real surroundings. Often Tati recorded his sounds in the natural setting of the countryside where people gather.

Realistic sounds blurt out disparate, yet precise signals.

Whenever possible Tati moves from the interior to the exterior of his settings, and vice versa, without disrupting human murmur. The talking in the kitchen in *Les Vacances* becomes a stream of words that can be heard outside in the empty square: *"Et un demi rosé. – Ça marche!"* ("Half a liter of rosé coming up!") Conversely, the cries from the beach (*"Reviens, tu es trop loin!"* ("Come back, you're too far out") flow unmodified all the way to Martine's house.

Space is continous. At least up to *Les Vacances*. With *Mon Oncle,* Tati starts to classify and isolate one space from another. He introduces sound as a way to establish borders, and then sets out to destroy these very borders.

The soundtrack used on the scene of the Saint-Maur market mixes accordion music and the cries of fruit and vegetable vendors. These sounds make their way into the telephone receiver in the S.D.R.C. boss's big, super-clean office (no longer as intact as it is in *Les Vacances*).

Playtime takes sound further still – all the way to sound-proofing. The glass pane shuts out noise, stamping it out completely.

Moving from the inside to the outside of scenes strengthens the montage of alternating sounds, which act like an articulated language linking one shot to another.

In *Trafic*, we ultimately surrender to a unified geography. During the bucolic sequences, the various noices made by the animals reshape the film's spatial unity. This is especially true in the episode about the country garage by the lake. Here, the chirping, mooing, and cackling overrun and gradually flood the film's reality.

10

The use of geography in Tati-World raises a number of questions.

Is the sky a place on which we cannot write? A wasteland? Do roads, those carefully-etched paths, exist in the sky? Is it only a question of straight lines? Or are we to interpret the sentence in *Jour de fête* – *"Là où finit la route le ciel continue"* ("At the end of the road, the sky begins") – as a celebration of flying straight as the crow flies?

Is the shortest path between two points – the line between points A and B – constraint or freedom?

Do the sky and the earth form two superimposed spaces (like a map juxtaposed on real territory), the juxtaposition of which creates freedom, movement, and space for dreaming?

On the ground level, we find arrows, beacons, and traffic lights.

Above: there is "free-flowing" traffic (free to take the shortest path) of planes, messages, radio waves.

What is the connection between the journey and the message?

CHAPTER 10

The Annunciation Made to Tati

"Oh c'est si pratique, tout communique."
("It's so practical; everything is connected.")
Mon Oncle

1

Let's now take a look at the presence of fish in Jacques Tati's films.

We'll start with the little gudgeon in the fisherman scenes of *Parade* and *Cours du soir*. The wriggling and struggling gudgeon that Tati tries to hold on to, slips away, and plunges back in the water.

But this is nothing compared to the other, more menacing fish: the shark that the commander sees through his binoculars, which is actually Hulot's kayak folded in two. In the last years of his life, Tati mentioned shooting a parody of *Jaws*.

Then there is the pike Hulot carries in his shopping basket at the beginning of *Mon Oncle* which, without his noticing, bares its teeth to a dog that breaks into a growling frenzy. (We have already seen two beasts, one dead and the other alive, with barred teeth in *Jour de fête*. Two foals in the meadow rear up when they catch sight of their wooden counterparts on the merry-go-round, staring back at them, jaws set in an eternal grin.)

What about the domineering fish, with gaping mouth, erected vertically in the Arpels' pond? The Arpels turn on the fountain-fish's jet only when an important guest comes to visit.

This terribly present and vocal fish whose too insistent presence upset Truffaut, we meet again, somehow sacrificed, stranded in a horizontal position on the serving dish at the Royal Garden restaurant. Here, it is offered under the name of "Turbot à la Royale," a culinary delight.

Though the turbot lies there, dead, and seasoned over and over again, no one will ever get to eat it. Isn't it really the only identified and personalized dish in the entire restaurant? This fish, which measures over fifty centimetres, cannot make it through the kitchen's narrow service hatch.

Yet it moves along. It swims in the water, and springs up, disappearing as quickly as our unconscious. The fish, which represents communication and its breakdown, is the star focus in two sweeping and brilliant passages.

The Arpels' fountain-fish in *Mon Oncle* is material for playfulness. Its jet shoots up, is cut off, goes back in, and fires up again, spoiled with blackened water. We can't help but think of scenes of childhood pissing competitions. Still, these images don't cancel the fact that gaiety, in Tati, is a secret code.

Who can forget the adventure stories about sailors crying "Thar she blows" every time an imposing whale is sighted?

The "jet" is a code. Its long-awaited presence signals the appearance of a mammal that dives and

reappears at regular intervals elsewhere in *Mon
Oncle*.

One evening Monsieur Arpel returns home
from work. His wife gently, in complicity says: *"Ne
fais pas de bruit, viens voir"* ("Don't make a sound,
come and see"), and leads him to their son's room.
Peeking through the half-open door, they rejoice at
seeing Gérard, seen from the back, at his desk,
deeply absorbed in a school book.

The scene is heart-warming: the couple   is
proud of their son.

As soon as the parents leave, the camera cuts to
a frontal shot, this time revealing what homework
their son is really working on. He has perfected a
pipe system that allows a jet of water to squirt out
of the sperm whale on the cover of his Natural Sci-
ences text book!

Yes, there is definitely an obsession with pipes
in this family!

Who is this gag aimed at? Who is it calling?

2

A man and a child are walking.

The man is holding the hand of a child who is
carrying a balloon.

The child pulls the coat sleeve of his father,
absorbed in reading the financial columns:
"Regarde, Monsieur Hulot!" (Look, it's Monsieur
Hulot!")

The father, fat Schmutz, doesn't bother to look,
content with patting his son's head distractedly.

This scene in *Les Vacances* echoes a scene in *Mon Oncle*.

Here is the essence of Monsieur Hulot, who acts as a vector, a link, a bridge that leads a child to his father.

The families in Tati's films are usually single-child families. Gérard Arpel is an only son, prone to boredom, whose parents, it would seem (in view of their apparent age), had him rather late.

Elsewhere, the girl of the Saint-Maur concierge is a single child as well.

The Schneiders in *Playtime* also have only one daughter.

It is later, in *Parade,* that the single boy (with his father) gets to meet the single girl (with her mother) at the circus.

Timid in his representations of young women, and more inspired by teenagers in pre-puberty or puberty (the concierge's daughter in *Mon Oncle*; the young Schneider girl in *Playtime*), Tati often celebrates young, astute fighters and practical jokers.

He denounces situations that frustrate a child, parents who cuff him for every little thing, and children who are obsessively pampered by wealthy parents.

At one point Gérard is left alone in the cold kitchen. We hear the distant voices of children playing.

Fade-out.

This is a rare example in Tati where the "off" sound is a call.

3

In *The Eclipse*, Monica Vitti whistles to a man in the
street; Alain Delon smiles.

Antonioni sends us back to Tati's famous scene
in *Mon Oncle*. The one where a group of boys, hiding on a hill above a street, mischievously whistle to
people walking below who turn their heads and
bump into a lamp-post they have not seen.

At the beginning of *Playtime*, a policeman's
rhythmic whistling attracts the attention of both
Barbara and Hulot who have not yet met.

The gym instructor whistles on the beach in *Les
Vacances*; Roger whistles after his dogs in *Jour de
fête*; Hulot is fired in *Trafic* because his boss blames
him for whistling (though he is not guilty).

People whistle to each other quite often in
these films. They whistle every opportunity they
get. Whistling is a language in the true sense of the
word. Men whistle to call one another; they whistle
to imitate a ship's siren (*Trafic*).

There is the beep-beep on intercoms. Men and
women hoot their car horns (*Les Vacances*).

With all this whistling going on, we would
expect more whistling in Playtime, a film about
modern society. On the contrary, there is little
whistling in this film. But that's precisely the point:
the rare whistling we do hear is so detached that it
becomes an obvious sign.

Unless the calls resound, amplified, as broadcast
voices coming out of loud-speakers, these sounds
generally neglect the logic of geography and pierce

right through the settings, transforming the space that carries them into an unreal element.

At times, these outbursts are the only real voices that convey a message.

In *Playtime*, female voices on phones neutralize the voice of the spider-like switch-board operator on her swivel chair in a labyrinth of offices.

In *Les Vacances*, a male voice announces unintelligibly which platform the trains are to arrive at, sowing confusion among the families gathered in the train station.

The Cerberus-like voices relay incomprehensible orders into the giant intercom of a building's entrance hall.

In *Trafic*, voices travel through space, just like the voices of the astronauts who landed on the moon and communicated with Earth.

Sitting in a shack by the lake, men and women listen to what the men on TV are saying. This is how juxtaposed worlds communicate with one another.

The air is saturated with messages and invisible wavelengths, intersecting, creating networks as real as our palpable world. Regardless of the voices, messages are silenced, important, decisive.

4

In one scene from *Trafic*, two workers carry a long plastic pipe, one at either end. The lazier man in front is daydreaming; he has stopped walking.

The one behind gives a jerk on the pipe which creates a tiny wave that grows into a warning signal for his colleague. As this wave is being transformed, an abstract sound whips through the air.

This quick visual gag symbolizes the most obvious form of telecommunication.

5

Tati introduces sounds that seem to contradict the unwavering clarity of his images. Fluctuation renders sounds present yet distant, precise yet muddled. Whatever sound fluctuates is entirely independent of the geographical logic of the visuals, that is, the position and movement of sound sources are not bound by the images.

This is most apparent in the way Tati manipulates human voices. By simply varying sound levels, he alternately makes one voice more predominant than another. (The voices are post-synchronized, recorded at close range.) Tati mixes sounds that allow for vocal close-ups, one sound overlapping the next within a single shot, respecting the position of every character. The spectator manages to isolate a phrase within the shot, yet does not necessarily know who, among the group, has spoken. Voices rise and weaken, as if the "reception" of the signal were actually fluctuating.

A similar quality is applied to sound effects, as in the case of footsteps. In *Playtime*, there is a shot which shows Giffard walking up a long corridor.

With implacably regular steps he makes his way
from the back of the screen up to the camera. On
the left of the frame, Hulot and the porter are waiting for him. The scene lasts several seconds, during
which the porter who, aware of how long it will
take, decides to smoke a cigarette.

   In this totally "expected" shot there is one thing
that doesn't seem normal: footsteps are the only
sounds we hear. The intensity of the heal-tapping
does not, however, increase linearly. On the contrary, the closer the sound gets, the lower the volume drops and and then suddenly up it jumps – all
carefully orchestrated.

   Naturally, while we are viewing the film, we are
neither aware nor bothered by this sound play. No
one is watching out for the footsteps in themselves.
This "fading" simulates, if you like, the perceptible
intermittence and variable investment of attention
in normal listening patterns, and has the effect of
boosting the suspense of the scene.

   Had the footsteps been linear, the sonorous elements would have sounded mechanical, as when we
hear noise that is regular and anticipated, we rapidly lose interest. In many ways, a fluctuating volume
in a fixed image kindles our interest.

   This "fading" has the effect of creating a basic
pulsation, a distinct rhythm of waves and wavelets
whose code is fundamentally binary. In general, we
could say that many aspects of a Tati film are ruled
by this binary code: action, the temporal continuity
(the jerky breaks between day and night scenes), the
depiction of characters, their being, Hulot himself,

whose existence depends on the strange play of appearing and disappearing. Every aspect of a film inscribes itself on both the microscopic and macroscopic levels.

6

Everything, absolutely everything, is made to stand out and follow a temporal rhythm. Every element starts and is interrupted, gets translated into long and short notation, much like the tapping of the Morse code.

A written Morse code: Hulot's footprints on the hotel staircase (*Les Vacances*) and on the desk where a lady from S.D.R.C. receives him (*Mon Oncle*); the telegraph knocks; the tooting and the unfailing discordant belches coming out of the Amilcar; the staccato bird song (*Les Vacances*).

A strident Morse code: the annoying clicking of Madame Arpel's heels; the rolling hum of the vacuum cleaner; the nervous unwinding of the winch (*Les Vacances*); the voluble hooting from the policeman's whistle (*Playtime*); the rough roar of the road drill (*Mon Oncle*); the turning on and off of the fish-fountain, its cracking jet; the neon light of the Royal Garden directing a drunk back to the bar, its flashing light thumping its telegraph signal.

A Morse code ribbon: the Plastac pipes popping out, afflicted with constrictions, swellings, varicose veins, resembling a secret code; a clumsy Hulot who

has involuntarily written on this tube a message that
he has to take somewhere. But to where?

The materiality of the message seems to mean
more than its content.

"Sending out messages is not my business:" this
is what some filmmakers reply, when accused of
making commercial films. "If you want a message,
ask the postman."

And isn't the protagonist of Tati's first full-
length film (and his last short-length film) precisely
that: a postman?

The two characters created by Tati have a lot in
common: they are links, bridges, and vectors carrying messages. Maybe this is why these two protagonists are always on the go.

That Hulot is "go-between" is not immediately
clear in the first film, but this becomes obvious by
the time we get to the second one. Hulot binds the
film together; he is the thread holding the scenes
together; his intermittent presence acts like the
weave in material; the scenes in which he does not
appear seem like a mass of erratic notations.

In *Mon Oncle*, Hulot is the one who goes to
pick up Gérard from school; he allows his nephew
to discover the neighborhood his family lives in.
Hulot is the one who, without being directly
responsible, will serve to bring father and son
together. (By whistling at a stranger Monsieur Arpel
triggers an incident that makes him his son's accom-
plice in this children's game.)

Hulot is given the function Tati would have
liked to play in society.

I'm so proud when I'm told that a son has asked his father a bunch of questions while watching my films (Quoted in *Jacques Tati*, by Penelope Gilliatt, Woburn Press).

What I want is for people to speak to one another when they're showing each other things (Interview in *Cahiers du cinéma*, No. 199, March 1968).

And so we arrive at this idea of films acting as intermediaries.

7

"Some news is so good that there's no hurry to get it," says an old lady in *Jour de fête*.

In view of her age, she is not too worried about the hazards involved in distributing mail. Still, there is that heap of letters awaiting delivery at the end of the film.

What do these letters say?

The apparent paradox in *Jour de fête* is that, though he makes the postman the protagonist of his film, Tati concentrates his gags less on the contents and the nature of the letters he delivers than on the act of delivering (or not delivering) the letters. When the content of the letter is mentioned, it is usually bad news. François hands a funeral card to the wrong person.

It is not clearly stated in *Playtime* either, whether the note Hulot is carrying concerns him – a letter of recommendation as we can, by linking it to *Mon Oncle*, reasonably suppose it to be – or if the note involves someone else altogether, in which case Hulot would then only be the "postman."

During the hide-and-seek sequence – Giffard and Hulot are running after one another in the building – there is a moment when they nearly meet. But then Giffard asks Hulot to wait, for he is busy giving instructions to another person, an employee who can't have a very good grasp of language – if we are to judge from the amount of precision that is necessary to draft a letter: "Send to, *ça veut dire que vous l'envoyez.*"

For once we are able to find a precise allusion to the content of the letter, but what does the letter deal with?

The act of sending information.

8

Tati's films speak (we've come to it now) about the wish to communicate, about the expectations a voice has when it calls you, about the attempts to return to a home barely hinted at.

What a complicated path we took in *Mon Oncle* to bring the hand of a child back to his father's! It is like the end of Bresson's *Pickpocket:* "What a long path to take to get to you."

The image isn't exactly similar. The essence of the Tati message is in this formula (write it down somewhere, if you like, and don't lose it): if you want to receive a message, you must not acknowledge it nor tell anyone you picked it up, for when this happens, mysteriously enough – that's how it is – communication breaks down.

The process itself by which the message is transmitted implies the closing off of something. Hulot is always doing nothing or listening to something happening elsewhere; the truth is that he is eager to receive a message.

Tati divides his film into distinct segments and, in doing so, through his gags, separates his spectators into subgroups. We laugh at different things, and rarely all together. This way there are fewer chances of having a collective and general reaction from the public, which would bring about a communication breakdown.

A division of elements aims at preventing a breakdown in communication. This system of interference in all Tati's works operates, on the one hand, within a specific film and, on the other hand, in what from one film to another changes and gets disturbed.

Every film cuts off elements that another began.

If we were to overlay all the maps and charts of the films together, we would get a splendid mess!

9

In *Playtime*, few company names can be read, underlined. There's just a handful of advertisements.

The city has a few signboards: *Drugstore, Salon de l'Auto*, of which only isolated letters are seen.

What does the viewer see? Written words, or more accurately, leftover words, more the debris of words than complete words, disjointed, crumbled pieces of words with missing letters: the "o" of "Drugstore" in *Playtime,* or the "o" of "Salon" in *Trafic*.

Absent letters.

Nothing else.

The seat is empty, waiting for a different set of signs, writing time that passes.

CHAPTER 11

A.R.

"Believe me, it's going to be very beautiful. I'm going to put spotlights all around the stage."
Playtime

1

The title of Tati's first short-length film is *OscAR, Champion de tennis*.

MARcel is the name of one of the fairground workers in *Jour de fête*, whose protagonist's first name is FRAnçois.

In *Les Vacances*, Hulot drives an AmilcAR. His partner is called MARtine, and BARbara is the name of the woman in *Playtime*. MARia is the name of one of the protagonists in *Trafic*.

The plot of *Mon Oncle* revolves around the ARpel family – such a wonderful name. The husband's first name is ChARles, and that of their only son is GérARd. Monsieur Arpel has a chief assistant called PichARd, who is the manager at Plastac.

In *Playtime*, besides BARbARa, we find the GiffARd family. It's Giffard whom Hulot wants to meet in the building. The only time they'll ever get to meet is by chance in the street in the evening.

We also meet Hulot's pal, MARcel, doorman at the Royal GARden.

The letters "a" and "r" light the title of Tati's last film, *PARade* – and before that *TRAfic*.

The title contains, in reverse order, the three letters A.R.T. AL*TRA*, the name of the firm Hulot works for. It is made up precisely of these three letters, to which an "L" is added.

"T" is both the initial letter of Tati and *Trafic*.

Just for sounds' sake, compare Jacques Tati (Tatischeff chose this as pseudonym) and his sister's name, Nathalie.

As for the "l" it is the only consonant – soft, feminine – audible in the name Hulot. The last letter, an unpronounced "t," is preceded by the letter "o," like the "o" we find in "Salon" – it is under that sign that Hulot will be sacked from Altra.

The blinding double "o"s recur in all Tati's films in the shape of the double oval windows of the Arpel residence.

How can one miss the double "o"s in Tati's mother's maiden name, Claire Van Hoof?

Two "o"s stare at you in the title *Mon Oncle*.

They are also visible in the title of a film which illness prevented Tati from making after *Trafic: Confusion*.

Mon Oncle: a title that sounds like a question: *mon nom* (my name?).

The film is about a woman who wants to find a wife for her brother Hulot. It also alludes to the Arpel's wedding anniversary.

Spell *mon nom(cle)* and you will become aware

of the silent "e" of the last syllable that hangs in midair.

It also reminds me of the first two consonants of Tati's mother's first name: *clé*, meaning *key*.

Hulot's name hints at the idea of possessing a home as well as having something to do with the mother's name or, if you wish, the mother's father's name – the name hanging outside a frame maker's shop, where Tati's father worked after he got married.

2

Tati's primary concern with the visuals of *Les Vacances* seems to be for images taken at the right distance, framed expressively from the accurate angle. He does not care for prettiness, which would not have worked in this film anyway. The beach paraphernalia is atrocious, the people vulgar. *Mon Oncle*, on the contrary, aims at beauty.

Tati justifies his position with reason and honesty. If he chooses to criticize the modern world, at least he doesn't do it through ugliness. Certain sequences in *Mon Oncle* – such as Arpel's journey to his factory, where there are only fragments of cars, radiators, indicators, and abstract manoeuvres – are motivated by concern for beauty and a search for pure plastic values, a search which, in *Playtime*, will come to the fore more forcefully. When speaking about *Playtime*, we spontaneously apply the adjective "beautiful."

Undoubtedly, this concern for beauty only appears in Tati when he decides to study the mod-

ern world. We may turn the question around and
ask ourselves if this interest in the modern world is
not just an excuse for Tati to measure himself
against beauty, by approaching beauty *ex nihilo*
(through his use of design), by inventing and building film-sets.

What is beautiful in Tati's films?

Certainly not the men and women; not even
those women we might consider pretty, charming,
and sweet. No, what is beautiful are the sets, the
composition, the forms.

Picture composition is an all important criteri-
um for Tati. It is as if he were placing a frame over
life.

Tati reserves his primary concerns with compositions for his characters first. Only later does he
apply it to the images that give his films such a
"contemporary" look. At times ridiculous, at times
excessive, his images are always beautiful.

Tati isn't a child of the theatre, nor is he a come-
dian who, though he does his job well, regrets having made people laugh. His concern for beauty is a
family matter.

We could ask ourselves whether beauty is
absolutely necessary to his films. *Les Vacances* is
totally successful without being either "beautiful"
or "ugly." Beauty is what stands out, like an add-on
value, self-sufficient.

What other message could Tati's films deliver
us, besides beauty?

3

The logos of the last three films (*Playtime*, *Parade*, *Trafic*) were designed by Tati himself. He uses them on posters and credits in such a way that they look like signatures or company trademarks. The care taken in creating titles that look like logos, giving them the same number of syllables as his own name, leads us to believe that, for Tati, his signature is essential: putting his name on a film is equivalent to a painter putting his signature on a painting.

Tati was the painter of films, the founder of a "firm."

Tati always claimed that he had complete "artistic freedom" while making his films. He introduced himself modestly, as the simple maker of funny movies, much like a cabinet maker would. This modesty, however, didn't prevent him from comparing his films to paintings.

Implicitly he spoke of *art* – a word which must have struck a sensitive chord in the Tatischeff-Van Hoof family. Love of art (and craftsmanship) justifies the waste of time and personal money he invested in polishing and re-polishing his films.

When Tati's father learned, to his regret, that his son had turned down the career of frame-maker (the job he himself had) to become an acrobat, Emmanuel Tatischeff could not have foreseen that his son would become an artist, in the best sense of the term.

Did he for one second think that his son's work would lead him to establish of a different type of "house" – a film-house or a production company?

Jacques Tati(scheff) had a number of good labels attached to his name; it was not difficult for him to be an artist.

Little effort was needed for him to sign his name as an artist does.

All he had to do was to place the letter "r" between the "a" and "t" of his surname.

CHAPTER 12

There's Evening, Then There's Morning

"Monsieur, il est l'heure, nous fermons."
("Sir, it's the last call.")

Playtime

1

A horse cart rolls by. A truck turns around the bend. A sports car darts off. Everybody's ready. This lasts no more, no less than the time it takes to shoot the scene. It's not made to be a burst of action, nor is it drawn out.

In a narrative film you would insert a typical transition shot to serve as a punctuation. According to the speed, the noise, the effect of movement in the field of action, it would be a comma, an exclamation mark, or a new paragraph. In this instance, what you have is a shot no different than the others. It is an image that exists entirely for itself, revealing whatever it is supposed to represent.

A car drives away in the evening.

Perhaps it is another time of the day – the afternoon. There is peace in the world.

If a war were to break out now, we would be able to say, upon watching a film by Tati, that it was shot in peace time.

2

World War Two, or what that war represented for
the French (the occupation, landings, occupiers,
and liberators), left its imprint on Tati's work.

In *Jour de fête*, the Allied forces are represented
by American GIs in a jeep, whom François wants to
impress. Americans are a haunting reference in this
film which Tati shot in 1946.

In *Les Vacances*, the hotel radio always trans-
mits Radio-London; a former commander recounts
his military exploits to anyone willing to listen.

Later, this military man will lead a column of
vacationers to a picnic, as though he were leading a
military attack.

During the costume-dress party, an official on
the radio delivers a solemn appeal to the country
and nobody listens.

At the end of the programme, we hear the Mar-
seillaise as everyone pushes off to bed.

Speaking of beaches: we cannot help but think
of the re-enactment of military landings that are
taking place as the hotel guests wake up to nocturnal fireworks involuntarily set off by Hulot.

To make the scene more effective and unambigu-
ous, Tati mixes the rumble of shellfire and explosions
with the roar coming from the pyrotechnics.

The military references are not as obvious in
Playtime, yet they are still present.

Tourists and business people come to Paris as if
they were landing in an occupied city.

3

Tati lived in an era of change. No wonder he always seemed to be out of step.

What Truffaut perfidiously wrote about *Mon Oncle* is still valid for *Playtime*:

> This is a film that talks about the present without showing it; two worlds are placed in opposition: one that existed twenty years ago; the other that we will live in twenty years from now (*Arts*, 1958, reprinted in *Les Films de la vie*, Flammarion, 1975, p. 258).

It is perhaps impossible for us to be witnesses of the present; we must first consider the present beyond its immediate and temporal limits.

Tati grants us a certain kind of evolution in *Trafic*. In *Playtime,* the young men and women – we say that an era is defined by its youth – have been eliminated almost entirely. The young appear sporadically and fugitively. What do you have but a few rockers strolling down a street? a transistor radio spitting out rhythms that end up disturbing even the gentle Barbara?

Tati makes up for the absence of young people in *Trafic* however. Here we have the sympathetic Dutch hippies whose values are celebrated.

In *Parade*, this celebration takes on the festive air of bell-bottom trousers, long hair, and psychedelic smoke, which is now visible not only in the public, but among the performers on stage as well.

4

You are listening to Radio-Cosmos.

With Radio-Cosmos we are tuned to the universe. From sunrise to sunset, Radio-Cosmos puts you in fleeting harmony with the rhythms of the world.

Radio-Cosmos doesn't broadcast grand, pompous music, but finely orchestrated melodies, light as wind.

Tati is tuned to this station. The soundtrack of his films contain the works of Jean Yatove, Alain Romans, Frank Barcellini, Francis Lemarque, James Campbell, Charles Dumont.

Music is never imposed on you: neither by the characters, nor by the director.

The music we hear comes directly from Radio-Cosmos.

With Radio-Cosmos you are tuned to the world.

Music is harmony, acceptance.

5

This is where "Once upon another time" clashes, despite all appearances, against "Once upon a time."

Time and time again, Tati repeats his gags and situations by treating them differently from film to film. In a few instances, there is an evening version and a morning version of the same gag.

In *Mon Oncle*, Hulot returns at night to the

Arpels and repairs the broken espalier he had begun repairing earlier. The unforgettable labyrinth staircase in Saint-Maur, where we see Hulot in long-shot going up and down the stairs, appearing, disappearing through all kinds of openings, has its nocturnal counterpart. It was filmed but unfortunately cut out at the final stages of putting the film together.

The sequence has Hulot returning home at night and struggling with the light switch.

In *Les Vacances*, tennis is presented twice. In the daytime, Hulot wins at tennis on the court; in the evening, he wins at ping-pong at the hotel. It's the same action, presented in variation.

Tati changes the time and space in which action takes place.

These films have no plotlines; there's no becoming. We sense a conscious refusal to end *Parade* in a decisive manner. Tati leaves the film open-ended and non-conclusive.

First there's morning, then there's evening. We are made slightly aware that it is not the same time of day, nor that it is the same air brushing against our skin. Such are the parameters of whatever it is that captures the single moment.

This is Tatian time that some critics (Bazin) consider incomplete and unfinished, and that others (Amengual) find perfect and closed.

If you want to give the impression that, no matter what happens, we are dealing with one and the same object, you might consider adding a variation, taking care not to allow this variation to alter the nature of the object.

Variations should lead neither to conclusions nor consequences. Variations on a theme should simply allow us to verify that we are still there, like when we blink at something seen.

The fact that *Les Vacances* follows *Jour de fête*, and that *Playtime* follows *Mon Oncle*, that *Parade* follows *Trafic* should not be mistaken as the organic result of the creative process (an improvement or a wish to attain perfection). Nor is this the normal outcome of pure contingency (creating with whatever means are at hand). If anything, it is the performance of an essential rhythm – exactly, like the blinking of an eye.

If Tati gives us morning and evening, it isn't to make us believe that he is leading us somewhere in particular. He wants to give life a chance to start all over again, even though it lacks any real sense of becoming.

Tati always wanted to make a film on imperceptible change.

Morning waits for you after you've thrown yourself, like a bundle of plastic, into the river at night.

6

Poetry rises from cars clogging up.

How do we end it all?

Cars gather in the town's traffic circle and create a jam. Traffic is hell, but a simple little trigger can release the enchantment, the music coming from a barrel organ. All can change.

This resounding music is what it takes to have

cars hopelessly turning in circles become part of a merry-go-round, going around metaphors that flourish and brighten our vision.

Unexpectedly a person drops a coin into the parking meter and the music starts all over again, as does the merry-go-round.

A child carries a balloon, and looks as though he is enjoying himself at a fair. Cars in a service station go up and down, just like toy cars.

Tourists in the bus notice the sky reflected in a glass pane that some worker tilts, and suddenly they feel like they are on a roller-coaster ride.

Isn't life a rapid jolt of events? An abrupt tilt of a window pane reflecting the blue sky which opens up to a dark drop below?

The fair begins today.

People are waiting. They don't look any happier than they did yesterday. They're simply not enjoying themselves. Tati reminds us how we have lost the means to enjoy themselves.

In *Jour de fête*, the village people never laugh. The only men and women who know how to laugh, albeit sardonically, are the fairground workers.

But, there again, they're only passing through.

No one knows how to have fun at a playground anymore.

It's time to celebrate.

What of it?

There's laughter in the air.

Orly-Paris, May/September, 1987.

FILMOGRAPHY

Shorts

1. *Oscar, Champion de tennis* (1932). Unfinished. Script and actor: Jacques Tati.

2. *On demande une brute* (1934). Director: Charles Barrois. Script: Jacques Tati, Alfred Sauvy. Assistant director: René Clément. Actor: Jacques Tati.

3. *Gai dimanche* (1935). 33 minutes. Dir.: Jacques Berr. Producer: Atlantic Film O.M. de Andria. Script: J. Tati and Rhum, the clown. Actors: J. Tati and Rhum, the clown.

4. *Soigne ta gauche* (1936). Dir.: René Clément. Prod.: Fred Orain (Cady Film). Script: J. Tati. Music: Jean Yatove. Actor: J. Tati.

5. *Retour à la terre* (1938). Script: J. Tati. Actor: J. Tati.

6. *L'École des facteurs* (1947). 18 minutes. Dir.: J. Tati. Prod.: Fred Orain (Cady Film). Script and dialogue: J. Tati. Ass. dir.: Henri Marquet. Photo.: Louis Felix. Music: Jean Yatove. Actor: J. Tati.

7. *Cours de soir* (1967). 30 minutes. Dir.: Nicolas Ribowski. Prod.: Specta Films. Photo.: Jean Badal. Music: Léo Petit. Actors: J. Tati, Marc Monjou.

Features

1. *Jour de fête* (1947). 70 minutes. Dir.: J. Tati. Prod.: Fred Orain (Cady Film). Script: J. Tati, Henri Marquet, with the help of René Wheeler. Adaptation: René Wheeler. Dialogue: J. Tati, H. Marquet. Photo.: Jacques Mercanton. Camera: Marcel Franchi, Citovitch, Mauride. Music: Jean Yatove. Prod. Dir.: F. Orain. Editing: Marcel Moreau. Clothes: Cottin. Set: René Moulaert. Actors: J. Tati (François), Paul Frankeur (Marcel), Guy Decomble (Roger), Santa Relli (Roger's wife), Maine Vallée (Jeannette), Roger Razal (Hairdresser), Beauvais (Bar owner), Delcassan (Old lady), Valy, Robert Balbo, and the inhabitants of Sainte-Sévère (Indre). Filmed between May 13 and November 15, 1947.

2. *Les Vacances de Monsieur Hulot* (1953). 96 minutes. Dir.: J. Tati. Prod.: Fred Orain (Cady-Films-Discina). Script: J. Tati, H. Marquet. Photo.: J. Mercanton, Jean Mouselle. Music: Alain Romans. Editing: Grassi, Ginou Bretoneiche, Suzanne Baron. Technical Advisor: H. Marquet. Ass. Dir.: Bernard Maurice, Pierre Aubert. Camera: Pierre Ancrenaz, Fabien Tordjmann, André Marquette. Prod. Dir.: Fred Orain. Régis gén.: Philippe Schwob. Acc.: Pierre Clauzel, André Pierdel. Actors: J. Tati (M. Hulot), Nathalie Pascaud (Martine), Louis Perrault (Fred), Michèle Rolla (Aunt), André Dubois (Commander), Valentine Camax (English woman), Lucien Frégis (Hotel manager), Marguerite Gérard (Walking lady), René Lacourt (Walking gentleman), Suzy Willy

(Female Commander), Raymond Carl (Boy), Michèle Barbo (Young female tourist), Georges Adlin (South American). Filmed between July 1951 and October 1952 at the Studios de Boulogne-Billancourt and at Saint-Marc-sur-Mer, near Saint-Nazaire, for outdoor scenes.

3. *Mon Oncle* (1958). 120 minutes. Dir.: J. Tati. Prod.: Specta Films - Gray Films - Alter Films (Paris) - Film del Centauro (Rome). Prod.: Louis Dolivet. Ass. Prod.: Alain Terouanne. Script: J. Tati. Artistic ass.: Jacques Lagrange, Jean L'Hote. Photo.: Jean Bourgoin (Eastmancolor). Sets: Henri Schmitt. Editing: Suzanne Baron. Music: Alain Romans, Franck Barcellini. Prod. Dir.: Bernard Maurice. Film Consultant: Fred Orain. Ass.: Henri Marquet, Pierre Etaix. Actors: J. Tati (Uncle Hulot), Jean-Pierre Zola (Monsieur Arpel), Adrienne Servantie (Madame Arpel), Alain Becourt (Gérard), Lucien Frégis (M. Pichard), Dominique Marie (Neighbor), Betty Schneider (Landlord's daughter), J.F. Martial (Walter), André Dino (Road Sweeper), Max Martel (Drunk), Yvonne Arnaud (Arpel's Maid), Claude Badolle (Ragman), Nicolas Bataille (Worker), Régis Fontenay (Strap Vendor), Adélaïde Danielli (Mme Pichard), Denise Péronne (Mlle Février), Michel Goyot (Car salesman), Francomme (Painter), Dominique Perly (Arpel's secretary), Claire Rocca (Monsieur Arpel's friend), Jean Rémoleux (Factory customer), Mancini (Italian salesman), René Lord, Nicole Regneault, Jean Meyet, Suzanne Franck, Loriot, Marguerite Grillières (Neighbor), and the inhabitants of Vieux Saint-Maur. Filmed at the studios of la Victorine and, for exterior scenes, in Créteil and Saint-Maur-les-Fossés.

4. *Playtime* (1967). 152 minutes, edited down to 137 minutes in February. Dir.: J. Tati. Prod.: Specta Films. Script: J. Tati with Jacques Lagrange. English dialogue: Art Buchwald. Photo.: Jean Badal (Eastmancolor – 70 mm). Sets: Eugène Roman. Music: Francis Lemarque. Theme song ("Take My Hand"): Dave Stein. African Music: James Campbell. Editing: Gérard Pollicand. Prod. dir.: Bernard Maurice. Prod. ass.: René Silvera. Ass. Photo.: Andreas Winding. Camera: Paul Rodier, Marcel Franchi. Actors: J. Tati (Monsieur Hulot), Barbara Dennek (Female tourist), Jacqueline Lecomte (friend of female tourist), Valérie Camille (Monsieur Lacs's secretary), France Rumilly (Eye glasses saleswoman), France Delahalle (Strand customer), Laure Paillette and Collette Proust (Two women with lamp), Erika Dentzler (Mme Giffard), Yvette Ducreux (Cloakroom woman), Rita Maiden (Mr. Schulz's friend), Nicole Ray (Singer), Luce Bonifassy, Evy Cavallaro, Alice Field, Eliane Firmin-Didot, Ketty France, Nathalie Jam, Oliva Poli, Sophie Wennek (Royal Garden customers), Jack Gauthier (Guide), Henri Piccoli (Important gentleman), Léon Doyen (Doorman), Georges Montant (Monsieur Giffard), John Abbey (Mr. Lacs), Reinhart Kolldehoff (German manager), Grégoire Katz (German salesman), Marc Monjou (False Hulot), Yves Barsacq (Friend), Tony Andal (Royal Garden manager), George Faye (Architect), Michel Francini (Royal Garden maître d'), Billy Kearns (Mr. Schulz), Bob Harley, Jacques Chaveau, Douglas Reed (Royal Garden clients), François Vaur (Royal Garden unfortunate client), Gilbert Reeb (Royal Garden playboy), Billy Bourbon (Bar plunderer).

5. *Trafic* (1971). 96 minutes. Dir.: J. Tati. Prod.: Robert Dorfmann. Script: J. Tati with J. Lagrange. Prod.: Films Corona (Paris), Gibé Films, Oceania Films (Rome), Selenia Films (Rome). Photo.: Edouard van den Enden, Marcel Weiss (Eastmancolor). Editing: Sophie Tatischeff, Maurice Laumain. Ass. Ed.: Marie-France Siegler, Alain Fayner, Roberto Giandalia. Prod. dir.: Marcel Mossoti. Actors: J. Tati (Monsieur Hulot), Maria Kimberly (Public relation person at Altra), Marcel Fraval (Truck driver), Honoré Bostel (Altra manager), François Maisongrosse (Altra salesman), Tony Kneppers (Garage man).

6. *Parade* (1973). 83 minutes. Dir.: J. Tati. Prod.: Gray Films, Sveriges Radio, CEPEC. Script: J. Tati. Photo.: Jean Badal, Gunnar Fischer. Music: Charles Dumont. Editing: S. Tatischeff, Per Carlesson, Siv Lundgren, Johnny Mair, Aline Fress. Camera: René Chabal, Jens Fischer, Bengt Nordwall. Artisic dir.: Jacques Lagrange. Ass.: Maire-France Siegler. Artsitic Advisor: François Bronett. Prod. man.: Louis Dolivet, Michel Chauvin. Exe. prod.: Karl Haskel. Actors: J. Tati (Monsieur Loyal), Karl Kossmayer and his donkey, the Williams family, the Veterans, the Argentinos, Johnny Lonn, Bertilo, Jan Swahn, Bertil Berglund, Monica Sunnerberg.

BIOGRAPHY

Tati's mother, Claire Van Hoof (1883-1969), was the daughter of the Dutch frame-maker who built Van Gogh's frames. The family eventually left Holland and settled in France.

Claire Van Hoof married Emmanuel Tatischeff (1875-1957), a frame-maker as well, son of Count Dimitri Tatischeff, a military attaché to the Russian embassy, and a French woman.

Claire Van Hoof and Emmanuel Tatischeff had two children: Jacques Tatischeff, born in Le Pecq, a suburb west of Paris, on October 9, 1908, and Nathalie.

Jacques Tatischeff had plans to study at the École des Arts et Métiers and take up the family trade. In the end fate led him to become a mime artist, much to his father's great displeasure.

As an amateur, Tati did impersonations of fishermen, tennis players, boxers, horse riders, and was quite successful.

He excelled in sports and became a fine rugby player. Yet in the end acting became his main passion.

Changing his name to Jacques Tati, he appeared in music-halls, such as Louis Leplée's "Gerny's," Théâtre Michel, and at the A.B.C., where writer Colette is said to have witnessed his talent. It was during one of these performances that Tati got the idea of filming his sketches.

This desire to make films led him to accept minor roles in shorts (the first being *Oscar, Champion de tennis*, 1932). He had a role in René Clément's *Soigne ta gauche* (1936) and also acted in two films by Claude Autant-Lara: *Sylvie et le fantôme* (1946) and *Le Diable au corps* (1947), where he makes a brief appearance as a soldier.

The magic moment came, however, in 1947, when Tati created François the postman who appeared in what would be Tati's last short film, *L'École des facteurs*.

Tati would later develop François for his first feature, *Jour de fête* (1947), produced by Fred Orain and filmed at Sainte-Sévère, in the Indre. Success for *Jour de fête* was slow to come, nevertheless it brought Tati enough money for him to shoot *Les Vacances de Monsieur Hulot* (1953), again with Fred Orain as producer.

Hulot came alive.

The international triumph of the film, especially in the U.S.A., helped Tati find the necessary backing to produce *Mon Oncle* (1958), which he filmed in better financial conditions.

From then on, Tati asked painter Jacques Lagrange to act as collaborator on his films. Together they worked on *Playtime*, *Trafic*, as well as *Parade*.

Shot both in French and English, *Mon Oncle* received a special mention at Cannes in 1958 and, in 1959, it won the Oscar for Best Foreign film in Hollywood.

In 1961, Tati presented his stencil tinted version of *Jour de fête* at the Olympia.

The highly anticipated *Playtime* came out in

1967. Shot in 70mm and with a whole town reconstructed on a wasteland near Vincennes, the film was not the success many expected.

Though admired by film buffs, Tati suffered the financial difficulties brought about by the failure of *Playtime*. It took the initiative of Dutch filmmaker, Bert Haanstra, before Tati could shoot *Trafic*, in 1971, resigning himself to using Hulot as the protagonist one more time.

In 1973, a Swedish television company helped Tati shoot *Parade*. Produced in video and later transferred into film, Tati was hoping to develop a new film form: musical comedy sketches played before a live Swedish audience.

Tati and Jonathan Rosenbaum were working on a film script entitled *Confusion*, when he passed away on the November 4, 1982.

Jacques Tati's artistic fate was paradoxical. Well-known and highly regarded in numerous foreign countries, he did only five full-length movies in thirty years.

Up to the end of his life, Tati refused numerous film offers (one of which was to produce an Italian *Totò et Tati*), with the excuse that such a film would have compromised his artistic integrity. Remaining faithful to his style was paramount to Tati.

In 1944, Tati married Micheline Winter and the couple had two children, Pierre and Sophie.

The latter, Sophie Tatischeff, became an editor and filmmaker in her own right. She has recently completed a documentary film dedicated to her father's career.

MEMBER OF SCABRINI MEDIA

Quebec, Canada
2003